A BOAT

a whale

&

A WALRUS

A BOAT

a whale

&

A WALRUS

· menus and stories ·

RENEE ERICKSON

with Jess Thomson

Photography by Jim Henkens · Illustrations by Jeffry Mitchell

SASQUATCH BOOKS
SEATTLE

Printed in China

Published by Sasquatch Books
18 17 16   9 8 7 6

Editor: Susan Roxborough
Project editor: Nancy W. Cortelyou
Writer: Jess Thomson
Photographs: Jim Henkens
Design: Anna Goldstein
Illustrations: Jeffry Mitchell
Copyeditor: Diane Sepanski

Library of Congress Cataloging-in-Publication Data is available.

ISBN: 978-1-57061-926-7

Sasquatch Books
1904 Third Avenue, Suite 710
Seattle, WA 98101
(206) 467-4300
www.sasquatchbooks.com
custserv@sasquatchbooks.com

For my parents, Jim and Shirlee

Table of Contents

Acknowledgments

There is an ocean of gratitude upon which every restaurant floats. And while a place's success may ebb and flow, that gratitude remains constant. I hope this cookbook inspires appetite and adventure, but I also hope you notice how these pages chronicle the people that have made my restaurants what they are today.

For understanding me, and for being patient, and for working hard, and for all the other things, I'd like to extend huge, hearty thanks:

To my parents, for always loving and supporting me. Mom and Dad, you are my biggest fans, hands down. Thank you for supporting me in all my crazy ideas. None of this would have happened without you.

To Ryan, Dolores, Maggie, and Mateo. Thank you for keeping the boat running, along with everything else. Ryan, you are the best brother a little sister could ask for.

To Dan, for loving me despite my crazy life and schedule. Your compassion grounds me and reminds me of all the good in this world.

To my co-author (and now dear friend), Jess Thomson. Thank you for keeping me organized, enduring so many pounds of butter, drinking rosé anytime of day, and never saying no to a Rainier tallboy. You are a fierce and lovely woman.

To my photographer and friend, Jim Henkens. I now understand your sense of humor, and the photos are perfect.

To my staff, past and present. Thank you for always keeping the restaurants running smoothly, but thank you especially for doing so when I was buried in these recipes. Special thanks to, in no particular order, Russell Flint, Marie Rutherford, Eli Dahlin, Bobby Palmquist, Jay Guerrero, Joe Sundberg, Shannon Haider, Erika Graczyk, David Little, and Robert Peterson, who make my days easier. And to Cody, who will always be remembered.

To my indefatigable and ever-inspiring business partners, Jeremy Price and Chad Dale. Jeremy, thank you for calling my bluff. Chad, thanks for always pushing. I couldn't imagine a better balanced trio, and I'm thrilled to be part of it.

To my godmother, Betty. Thank you for sharing your cabin with me.

To my favorite farmers, suppliers, and purveyors, to whom I grant my trust and much of the responsibility for my restaurants' successes.

To my mentors in food, wine, business, beauty, and sensibility: Patricia Wells, Carrie Omegna, Susan Kaplan, Jeffry Mitchell, and Curtis Steiner. I carry parts of you with me each day.

To the handfuls of recipe testers who helped Jess comb through each recipe carefully, to make sure we've given you all the information you need.

And last but not least, to the crew at Sasquatch Books, for seeing our vision for this project through to the end. It's been a tasty project, to say the very least, and you allowed me to make it so, so beautiful.

Introduction

At first, I was a twentysomething who owned a little French-inspired restaurant in Seattle's University District. I worked the way all new restaurant owners do—every moment my eyes were open. My mom made desserts and my dad peeled potatoes. My brother fixed everything that broke. That restaurant, Boat Street Café, taught me that I loved to cook for people, and that I'd be happy pouring the rest of my life into a living, breathing business that provides guests with excellent food-and-wine experiences day after day after day. Then, quite unexpectedly, I was forced to close it.

I spent a difficult two years in limbo before reopening the café in a better spot, with more freedom but some of the same fantastic staff. Five years and a much-appreciated popularity boom later, I began trusting the kitchen to other chefs. With a tenacious business team, I opened three more restaurants: The Walrus and the Carpenter, The Whale Wins, and, most recently, Barnacle. Somewhere along the way, between late nights and birthday parties, I realized I'd made my business work. And more than anything, I realized I'd done it with the help of the people who surround me at the restaurants every day—my friends, my family, and my staff. So I decided to write a cookbook to celebrate.

One day, I spread a sheet of butcher paper out on the bar at The Whale Wins. I divided the year into four seasons, simply because that's how I cook, and mentally scanned the dinners that define my life and my restaurants' personalities. I made a scratchy list of the foods I consider crucial pillars of my cooking style— old favorites, like the chicken liver pâté I learned to cook at Boat Street Café before I bought it from Susan Kaplan in 1998, and new staples, like wood oven–roasted chicken and herring butter. I took stock of my best travel memories. I thought about the people who have helped make my restaurants what they are today. And suddenly, almost magically, there was the outline of a cookbook in front of my eyes—an edible, celebratory diary of how I live, both in my restaurants and at my home. This book is a collection of my favorite menus.

It also shares the experiences I have as a restaurant owner every day, highlighting the people who work for me, the farmers who grow food for our restaurants, and the guests who visit. I am honored and proud to have it all—my staff especially. I hope you cook through this book as you please, calling friends together to enjoy the menus as they're presented, patching together your favorite mix of dishes, or simply reading these pages, putting the book down, and wandering into the kitchen.

Renee Erickson

Who We Are

THE STYLE

In general, my restaurants are energetic but quiet. I think the mood is probably set by me; I'm a relatively calm person and I never stay mad, which means I can air my grievances and move on. I think that's an important trait in a kitchen, and it keeps things peaceful, which translates to relaxed customers.

I'm also not a classically trained chef—actually, I'm not trained at all—so there aren't a lot of rules about cooking in my kitchens. It's more important to me that people are happy and comfortable than that they can crack an egg with one hand or slice a case of shallots in a minute flat. If I don't want to do something, I don't want to make someone else do it. I want my staff to have healthy lives and dynamic, interesting jobs that don't entail someone hovering over them.

I think my kitchens are also a bit unique because they're run by a woman. There's a classic chef ego that comes out of France that's often associated with the French-inflected food we cook. By and large, women aren't really allowed in fancy French kitchens, so there can be an intimidation factor involved in cooking French food if you're a female chef. I don't have the time or energy to play those games, and I'm not trying to train my cooks to be perfect, like some owners do. There are no *tournéed* potatoes in my restaurants. There is no fussy presentation. Starting with Boat Street Café, my first restaurant, I decided that the food I cooked didn't need to match everything about that food's history, which enabled me to develop my own cooking and managing style.

As a whole, my four restaurants are individual spots, but they're also a network of related kitchens, like culinary siblings that live across town from one another but see each other every other day. They have a strong common thread—me—but each has its distinct personality. My goal as an owner has been to recognize the strengths of a given chef and allow him or her to run with those skills. As a result, I have four very different babies.

THE RESTAURANTS

Boat Street Café
In the spring of 1998, after working for owner Susan Kaplan for about four years, I bought Boat Street Café, then located on Boat Street near Seattle's Portage Bay. It was a quaint little neighborhood spot, a place frequented by professors,

BARNACLE

artists, and Francophiles, where you could get a good roast chicken and smooth pâté served with pickled prunes and a great glass of French wine. In 2003 landlord issues caused the restaurant to close, but I reopened it in the fall of 2005 on Western Avenue, sharing a kitchen with a separate restaurant called Boat Street Kitchen. It was an iteration of its predecessor, a design project shared with Susan. The light, airy space has always been the physical incarnation of my artistic style. It has the strongest French accent of my four restaurants. Boat Street is where I grew up as a cook, and as an artist. It's where I learned about my love of travel, wine, and food. It's the place that friends and family call their favorite, and it's where all of my head cooks have started.

The Walrus and the Carpenter

In August 2010, after forming a business relationship with Chad Dale and Jeremy Price, I opened The Walrus and the Carpenter, an oyster bar in Seattle's Ballard neighborhood. Initially, it was inspired by the oyster bars of Paris, but I wanted something more adventurous. Named after characters in the whimsical 1871 Lewis Carroll book, *Through the Looking-Glass, and What Alice Found There*, in which the two protagonists come upon a crowd of personable oysters and eventually decide to eat them all, the busy bar focuses on all foods fishy, from smoked trout to herring butter to, yes, local oysters. Inside, it's the Seattle cross between an old seaside fish shack and a Parisian bar, a place to come to quaff a perfect glass of muscadet with a fresh dozen, or to nibble on butter clam tartare and cured duck breast. In June 2013, Walrus, as we call the restaurant, spawned a mobile oyster and catering truck called Narwhal.

The Whale Wins

On Halloween 2012 my business partners and I opened The Whale Wins. A year before, I'd purchased a painting with the same title, in which a giant blue whale knocks two whalers out of their boat. Based on food that either emerges from a central wood-fired Italian marble oven or is served at room temperature, it has a highly seasonal, produce-focused menu and a bright, airy atmosphere that's simultaneously welcoming and impressive. Look up if you're sitting in the main part of the dining room; the lights spell "Hello Hello."

Barnacle

Ages before we opened Walrus, Jeremy Price, in his infinite wisdom, decided we'd someday own a bar called Barnacle. We didn't know then that it would be such an appropriate name for the tiny small-plates spot we opened just next to Walrus. With fantastically charming co-owner David Little at the helm, Barnacle celebrates bright fish dishes—cured, smoked, and canned fish—along with house-made charcuterie and local cheeses. Creative cocktails, *amari*, and incredible Italian wines round out the menu.

The Owners

In 2008, when Chad Dale was working on developing the Kolstrand Building in Seattle's hip Ballard neighborhood, he needed a restaurant tenant. When he approached me at Boat Street Café with an idea, I turned him down. Later, after a string of yeses and nos, I turned him down again because I was terrified of expansion. Eventually, because he is persistent and smart, and because he has a magnetic personality I gravitated toward, I agreed to look at the space. When he showed me the hidden little gem at the back of the building that now houses The Walrus and the Carpenter, I joked that I might someday be interested. He called again the next day, and we agreed to go into business together.

When I decided to open a second restaurant, I was daunted. (It's a feeling I've since gotten used to having after conversations with Chad and Jeremy Price, our other partner, about new projects.) I couldn't imagine having the energy I poured into Boat Street Café in double; I knew I needed a general manager with a ferocious sort of energy, someone who would be tenacious in the face of criticism and willing to work ten thousand times as hard as any human should. I picked Jeremy, a longtime Boat Street employee, because he'd once had the courage to tell me, right out loud, that he'd like to own a restaurant with me someday. He said he had the eye of the tiger, like in that old Survivor song, and I held him to it.

Since then, our little ownership trio has worked amazingly well, especially considering how little we knew each other before, say, 2009. We are all compulsive workers—for better or worse—which means we all trust each other to do whatever it takes to perform our assigned jobs. I am generally the figurehead and I think about food and buy the wine; I manage the chefs and coordinate new menus. Jeremy is the practical one who handles all the nitty-gritty details; from payroll to new construction, he is the day-to-day operations guy. (He also happens to have a crack eye for designing restaurant spaces, which has come in handy.) Chad handles investments and looks out for our interests, interacting with landlords and neighbors and helping us make the best decisions about what comes next.

Methods

HOW TO USE THIS BOOK

You'll Have Extra

I believe in leftovers. These recipes make the amount of food I'd serve at my own home, but know that I am a restaurant cook. I like to open the fridge and remember the previous day's work, in the form of a bite of a savory butter spread on toast, or a wisp of dessert that I can sneak into a bowl next to my morning coffee. I also eat more than most people, perhaps because I'm used to restaurant-size portions. So dig in, and expect to save some for later occasionally.

Buy Good Food

That I am uncompromising when it comes to choosing ingredients is not exactly news; I've built a decent business on sticking to my guns. In the kitchen, that means using only the very best I can find, from crab to cognac to crème fraîche. I suggest you do the same, which is why I've included a resource list (page 293) for purchasing everything from salt and olives to pickles and Padrón peppers. Yes, you're right, good food is more expensive than bad food. I'd rather eat very simply on a regular basis so I can eat well at the parties described in this book.

Find a Boat

You might also notice that, if you're going to follow many of the recipes in this book to the letter, it will be convenient to have a friend with a boat. For me, the summers in Puget Sound are ripe with salmon, crab, and spot prawns, and I like to celebrate these creatures in my restaurants as much as I can—and fish for them whenever I'm not running a business. I encourage you to make the catch part of the feasting experience.

The Way I Cook

This book assumes you know your way around the kitchen relatively well. As a whole, these recipes are accurate, but they're not as exacting as your own taste buds. In the restaurants, we taste and test our food every time we cook it. You should too. Seasoning your food the way you like it is what's most important.

Charring Food

Although most kitchen horror stories involve burning things, in my mind, it's a much more serious offense to not cook food *enough*. When meats and vegetables come into contact with searing heat, something magical happens; the sugars in the foods caramelize and new flavors are born. In this book, when I talk about charring food—for, say, Grilled Bread (page 277) or Roasted Carrots and Fennel (page 263)—I mean that the edges of the food should be very, *very* dark brown. When cooking vegetables, you need to not touch them. The more a vegetable is moved, the more liquid is released, and the more they steam instead of brown. Ditto for meats. When grilling toasts, put a heavy pan on top of them, which ensures the bread lies directly on the grill. Don't smash them—you're not making panini—but you do need to grill them until they're almost black and just beginning to smoke. Do I burn things? Sure. In my kitchen, the line between properly cooked and burned is relatively thin. And that's just the way I like it.

Choosing Olive Oil

In many recipes, I call for *finishing oil*, as opposed to just an extra-virgin olive oil. These are great oils whose delicate flavors might be masked by the cooking process; they're only to be used directly from the bottle. (They usually come in fancier bottles, with fancier price tags.) I also sometimes differentiate between types of great extra-virgin olive oils. A *buttery* or *soft* olive oil is made from darker olives, such as those found in France or Italy's Liguria region. A *sharp* or *grassy* olive oil is more typical of Tuscan or Spanish olives. In general, pair simple flavors with sharper oils, and more complicated flavors with softer oils. (Remember that heat and light kill an oil's flavors, so good olive oil should never be kept next to the stove.)

Cleaning Mushrooms

Since mushrooms live in the forest, where it rains, I'm not afraid to wash them. However, I'm always gentle. I typically set the mushrooms in a bowl and add water to cover, then jostle them with my hands to release the dirt. I let the dirt settle to the bottom of the bowl for a few minutes, then lift the mushrooms out and transfer them to a towel to dry, leaving the dirt in the bottom of the bowl. For foraged mushrooms, like morels and chanterelles, I often repeat this process multiple times if they're extra dirty.

Crushing Sea Salt

Although I use multiple types of salt, I'm not a big fan of having an entire counter full of salt boxes. I typically have just two types of sea salt: either Maldon, Jacobsen, or another flaky sea salt, and a gray sea salt, such as *sel de Guérande* (see Resources, page 293). I use it as is, or, if I want smaller pieces, I just crush it between my fingertips to make it smaller. If I want ground sea salt, I grind it myself in a mortar and pestle, because I can control the texture best that way.

Measuring Flour

At my restaurants, we almost always weigh our flour, because it's the only way to achieve perfect consistency in baked goods. At home—and for this book—I use the scoop-and-sweep method, dipping a measuring cup into a bag of loosened flour and leveling the cup off with the flat side of a knife. (If you'd like to be very accurate, weigh your flour.)

Picking Herbs

When I call for fresh herbs, I occasionally use them chopped, but more frequently, I use the leaves whole, without the stem. To pick herbs, keep them refrigerated until the last minute, then wash them gently in a bowl of cold water, shake to remove excess water, and dry gently on a clean towel. Carefully remove each individual leaf, discarding the stem. If I need to pick a large amount of parsley, for example, and it makes sense to do it a bit ahead of time, I line a container with a moist paper towel, gently pile the cleaned, picked herbs on top, and cover them with another moist paper towel until I'm ready to use them.

Reviving Herbs

The downside of using lots of herbs for flavor is that you have to keep track of their freshness. If soft herbs (such as parsley, tarragon, chervil, or cilantro) are looking a little lackluster, trim the stems and plunge the whole bunch into a bowl of cold water. Let them soak until they start looking a bit more energetic.

Serving Food at Room Temperature

Although we've all been admonished for letting hot food get cold, I'm a big fan of serving food at room temperature on purpose. It has two main advantages: first, I think it's the temperature at which a dish's flavors can be the most complex, and second, it means you can serve a large group easily. I dare you.

Toasting Nuts

I toast nuts on a sheet pan in a 350-degree oven. The amount of time required depends on the type of nut, but the result should be the same: about 10 minutes into toasting, you should start to smell the nuts. (Set a timer every time, even if you think you'll instinctively smell them.) The scent means the nuts are close to done; they are toasted when every nut is a full shade darker than when they started, and the skins crackle audibly. (I love tossing toasted nuts with butter and salt before using them, like in the Butter Lettuce Salad on page 123.)

Toasting Spices

The fresher the spice, and the more recently toasted, the more flavorful, which is why I always toast and grind spices like fennel, coriander, caraway, and cumin whole, and then grind them myself in a mortar and pestle. To toast spices, put them in a small skillet over medium heat and cook, shaking the pan occasionally, for three to four minutes, or until the seeds are a shade darker in color and they begin to perfume the room.

Using Citrus Peel

The vibrant, waxy portion of a citrus fruit—technically called the zest—is filled with aromatic oils that lend foods a bright, floral flavor and aroma I can't live without. In this book, I use it in three different ways: finely grated, julienned, or stripped. In all cases, you should use just the colored portion of the citrus zest, not the bitter white pith underneath. To finely grate citrus zest, rub the fruit against the sharp side of a Microplane grater. To julienne the peel, either use a dedicated citrus zester, or use a vegetable peeler to first remove an inch-wide strip from the citrus, then a sharp knife to cut the peel into razor-thin slices. To strip citrus (typically for cocktails or braises), just use a vegetable peeler to remove a strip of the peel. See My Favorite Tools (page 14) for more information.

Using Preserved Lemons

I use preserved lemons frequently in cooking, because they impart a savory flavor and lovely citrus perfume to anything they're added to. Although many cooks use the whole lemon, I usually use just the peel, rather than the entire lemon. To use just the peel, first soak the lemon in a bowl of water for an hour or so, changing the water once or twice along the way. Rinse the lemon well and cut it into quarters vertically. Then simply slide your thumb between the peel and flesh of each piece, so you have four empty strips of lemon peel. (Discard the flesh.) Press each piece flat on a cutting board, then use a small paring knife to trim the clear pith from the peel. Use as directed, usually in very thinly sliced strips (julienne).

Tools

MY FAVORITE TOOLS

Below is a list of the tools I rely on. It is by no means exhaustive, but they're tools that I believe every well-stocked kitchen should have.

Butcher's twine
USED FOR: Tying roasts together
LOOK FOR: The kind that stands up on its own, rather than a ball

Canning jars
USED FOR: Canning, storage
LOOK FOR: Jars with washable seals, such as Weck (WeckJars.com)

Cast-iron pan
USED FOR: Searing meat, roasting, baking
LOOK FOR: Something heavy, such as Lodge (LodgeMfg.com)

Citrus zester
USED FOR: Removing thin strips of zest from citrus fruit (not grating it)
LOOK FOR: Something that feels comfortable in your hand

European-style (also known as Swiss) vegetable peeler
USED FOR: Peeling vegetables, stripping lemon zest
LOOK FOR: A lightweight, durable Y-shaped version, such as Kuhn Rikon (KuhnRikon.com)

Fine-mesh strainer
USED FOR: Making cheese, straining sauces
LOOK FOR: Something with a sturdy handle and hooks that let you balance it over a bowl

Gratin dishes
USED FOR: Making gratins, roasting vegetables
LOOK FOR: Lots of different sizes, from a brand like Le Creuset (LeCreuset.com)

Grill pan
USED FOR: Grilling meat, grilling bread
LOOK FOR: Coated cast iron, from a brand like Le Creuset (LeCreuset.com)

Heavy-duty blender
USED FOR: Making vinaigrettes and mayonnaise, blending soup
LOOK FOR: Something that can hold large volumes, like a Vitamix (Vitamix.com)

Instant-read thermometer
USED FOR: Measuring temperature
LOOK FOR: Taylor brand
   (TaylorUSA.com)

Kitchen scale
USED FOR: Weighing meat, fish, and
   produce
LOOK FOR: Something you have room
   for on your counter, such as the
   small scales made by Salter
   (SalterUSA.com)

Knives
USED FOR: Cutting, dicing, chopping,
   slicing
LOOK FOR: Good carbon steel, such as
   Korin (Korin.com)

Mandoline
USED FOR: Slicing vegetables
   extremely thinly
LOOK FOR: A thin mandoline with
   interchangeable blades, such as
   Benriner (Benriner.com)

Microplane grater
USED FOR: Finely grating citrus peel,
   ginger, and horseradish
LOOK FOR: Microplane brand
   (Microplane.com)

Mortar and pestle
USED FOR: Pounding sea salt, grinding
   spices
LOOK FOR: A small, heavy marble one
   that fits on your counter

REAL TOWELS

I'm a fan of towels—not the paper kind, but real cloth towels, the kind you hang from your oven door. At home, I keep a huge wicker bin of them next to my oven, and I use them in lieu of paper towels, to mop up messes, blot food, and soak up excess liquid wherever it appears. I accumulate them when I travel, mostly, but especially in Parisian antique markets. They're pretty, and they're washable. And because living in the restaurant world inevitably means making a lot of waste, it makes me feel good to use a little less paper at home. Feel free to use cloth wherever paper is suggested in this book.

WINTER

Wintry Brunch

Boat Street Cream Scones *20*
Blackberry Jam, Butter

House-Smoked Salmon *25*
Brown Sugar Brine, Capers, Crème Fraîche, Rye Toasts

Strata *29*
Button Mushrooms, Cheddar, Leeks, Dill

Spicy Pork Crépinettes *31*

Butter Lettuce Salad *(page 123)*
Toasted Pistachios, Green Herbs, Sheep's Milk Cheese

Molasses Spice Cake *36*
Whipped Cream, Candied Orange Peel

SERVES 12

I LOVE THE NOISE AND THE RUMBLE and the laughter that emerge when people eat together, which is one reason I love restaurants. Historically, I think people ate at home together more than we do now. Over time, we've accidentally fallen out of the habit of sharing our food. Today, restaurants in general fill that gap. I like to serve shared plates because I think it's a more normal, more natural way of eating.

I have friends who like making artful dishes at home, but frankly, that's not how I cook. I cook as a means of hearing what's happening in peoples' lives, so I don't want the food to steal the show. The people are simply more important; I can cook 'til I'm blue in the face, but if no one's around to eat it, and form a community around it, it's just a bunch of food.

boat street cream scones

blackberry jam, butter

PREP TIME: 20 MINUTES // TOTAL TIME: 40 MINUTES // MAKES 12

WHEN I FIRST BEGAN COOKING AT Boat Street Café, I started baking scones for our weekend brunch. It was a good place to learn for someone who wasn't fast but could pay close attention to details. Susan Kaplan taught me to fold them gently and shower them with just the right amount of crunchy sugar. At home, on a wintry Sunday morning, scones are buttery and sweet and all that good business, but for me, they're mostly a vehicle for excellent jam. And I always have excess cream in my refrigerator, so on a Sunday morning when I wake up hungry, they're my go-to when I know friends might stop by.

4 cups (about 512 grams) all-purpose flour, plus more for forming scones
½ cup granulated sugar
2 tablespoons baking powder
½ teaspoon kosher salt
½ cup dried currants
Grated zest of 2 large lemons

2 cups plus 2 tablespoons heavy cream, divided
2 tablespoons demerara sugar (see Resources, page 293)
Unsalted butter, for serving
Blackberry Jam, for serving (recipe follows)

+ Preheat the oven to 400 degrees F. Line a baking sheet with parchment paper and set aside.

+ Sift the flour, granulated sugar, baking powder, and salt into a large mixing bowl, then whisk in the currants and lemon zest. Slowly add 2 cups of the cream to the dry ingredients, stirring it in with a large fork just until a dough forms. Using floured hands, pat the dough together a few times to encourage it to hold together, then transfer it to a floured surface. Divide the dough into 2 parts and form each into a disk roughly 6 inches in diameter and 1 inch tall. Using a large, sharp knife, cut each disk into 6 equal wedges. Brush the tops of the scones with the remaining 2 tablespoons of cream, then sprinkle them with the demerara sugar.

+ Using a spatula, transfer the wedges to the prepared baking sheet. Bake the scones for 15 to 20 minutes, or until they are puffed and their tops are browned. Serve immediately, slathered with butter and blackberry jam.

blackberry jam with fresh bay

PREP TIME: 30 MINUTES // TOTAL TIME: 30 MINUTES, PLUS COOLING TIME
MAKES ABOUT 4 CUPS

IF I HAD TO PICK A favorite summer berry, I'd pick blackberries every time. And if I had to pick a favorite jam, it would be blackberry jam—it's tart and only as sweet as absolutely necessary. Give the extra to friends, or can it properly according to your canning jar manufacturer's instructions.

The cooking time for this jam will depend on the berries you use; you want a mixture that sets in the freezer after a minute or two. Note that the jam will thicken considerably upon standing.

NOTE: If you don't have fresh bay leaves, substitute a big sprig of fresh thyme or, if available, anise hyssop.

3½ pounds ripe summer blackberries (about 8 half-pint baskets) or 4 (10-ounce) bags frozen organic blackberries

3½ cups plus 1 tablespoon sugar
⅓ cup freshly squeezed lemon juice (from about 2 large lemons)
3 fresh bay leaves

+ First, place a few small plates in the freezer. You'll use these to test the jam for doneness.

+ Combine the berries, sugar, lemon juice, and bay leaves in a large nonreactive pot. (You want to cook the jam at a hard, rapid boil, so that the liquid evaporates quickly, so use the widest pot you have, even though this batch of jam isn't so large.) Over low heat, cook, stirring, until the sugar melts. Increase the heat to high. Cook at a hard boil, skimming off any foam with a spoon, for about 20 to 25 minutes, stirring frequently. (Mother the jam a bit here; it's best to cook it as fast as you can, but also important to turn the heat down briefly if it boils up to the top of your pan.) Since both stoves and berry juiciness differ, it's important to test the jam for doneness; you'll know the jam is ready when a teaspoon of it gels on a frozen plate in a minute or two.

+ When the jam is done, remove and discard the bay leaves. Ladle the jam into 4 cup-size jelly jars, seal them according to the jar manufacturer's instructions, and let them cool to room temperature. Store at room temperature, properly sealed, up to 6 months, or up to 1 month in the refrigerator once open.

house-smoked salmon

brown sugar brine, capers, crème fraîche, rye toasts

PREP TIME: 10 MINUTES // TOTAL TIME: 10 MINUTES // SERVES 12

EVERY TIME I GO TO NEW YORK, I go to Russ & Daughters, the Jewish food institution on the Lower East Side. It's important to pay attention from the moment you walk through the door. Just inside, there are big wooden vats of fermenting pickles. You have to glance at the pickles quickly, then push your way in to take a number before your eyes wander across the caviar and bagels, and you lose yourself in the way the men behind the counter delicately trim each piece of pickled and smoked fish before packing it up. It's a step back in time, that store, and it seems that it can only exist in New York. When I long for something similar in Seattle, I give up the dream of replicating their horseradish cream cheese and make a smoked salmon platter for brunch.

NOTE: If you don't want to smoke your own salmon, buy hot-smoked salmon (the flaky kind), not lox (the slippery kind), for this platter.

---

2 fillets Jimmy's House-Smoked
  Salmon (recipe follows)
½ red onion, very thinly sliced
½ cup capers (salt-packed preferred), rinsed well (see Capers,
  page 188)

1 cup crème fraîche
1 lemon, cut into 12 slices
3 dozen Rye Toasts (page 278)

✦ Arrange the salmon, onion, capers, crème fraîche, lemon slices, and toasts on a big platter and serve.

jimmy's house-smoked salmon

PREP TIME: 30 MINUTES // TOTAL TIME: ABOUT 24 HOURS
MAKES 4 (ROUGHLY ½-POUND) SMOKED SALMON FILLETS
SPECIAL EQUIPMENT: STOVETOP SMOKER

ALTHOUGH THE CONSEQUENCES OF SMOKING FISH improperly are serious—I recommend consulting a good smoking cookbook for full instructions—the process of smoking your own catch is, in my experience, one of the most rewarding benefits of living in the Pacific Northwest. Rather than the often chemical-infused taste of store-bought smoked salmon, the homemade version really only has three flavors: salmon, sweetness, and smoke.

continued

The problem with smoking salmon, I'll admit, is that it instills in me a sometimes dangerous sense of adventure. One of the first times I smoked salmon whole, I traipsed up to photographer Jim Henkens's house on Lummi Island, where he has a giant cedar smokehouse in his backyard. I brought six huge king salmon, filleted and brined, and decided that instead of following Jim's traditional flat-drying technique, I wanted to hang my fillets to dry, like the area's Native Americans have for years. (The back of Jim's old house is fitted with nails we suspect were used decades ago for that very purpose.) Drying the salmon gives it the slightly parched, shiny skin characteristic of smoked salmon.

Rain prevented us from hanging the salmon to dry outdoors, as was planned, so Jim rigged a piece of wood flooring up high in his basement to serve as a drying rod. Along with Bobby Palmquist, now the chef at Barnacle, we nailed the giant, heavy king salmon fillets up to the wood late at night with ¾-inch galvanized nails, all lined up like pink soldiers. In the morning, we woke to find the poor fish had dropped overnight onto the tarp we'd spread on the ground, their own weight too much for their tails to hold. Note to self: Always hang salmon whole, supported by the tough cartilage in their mouths, not by their tails. I've gotten much better at smoking whole salmon since then.

This version is much more tame and should be easy to do at home with a small countertop smoker. It's a scaled-down version of Jim's old reliable recipe. It also takes less time, although the exact time will depend on the thickness of the fish you use. Pink salmon is the more traditional species to smoke, but since king fillets are almost always thicker, they are less apt to dry out. Choose what looks best to you (or what ends up on your hook), but note that the smoking time given here isn't set in stone.

½ cup kosher salt

¼ cup light brown sugar

¼ cup organic granulated sugar

1 tablespoon finely chopped fresh thyme

1½ teaspoons freshly ground black pepper

4 (8-ounce) king or pink salmon fillets, of roughly even thickness

¼ cup (½ stick) unsalted butter, melted (optional)

2 tablespoons cognac or brandy (optional)

½ cup fine alderwood or cherry-wood chips

✦ In a mixing bowl, whisk together the salt, brown sugar, sugar, thyme, and black pepper to blend. In a large stainless steel or glass pan, mix the salmon fillets with about half of the salt mixture, then arrange the salmon in a single layer and top with the remaining salt. Cover and refrigerate for 4 to 6 hours.

✦ Next, line a baking sheet with paper towels and place a cooling rack on top. Rinse the fish thoroughly under cold water, then spread the fillets out again, skin side down, on the rack. Let the fish dry, uncovered, in the refrigerator for 10 to 12 hours. This is when the fish forms the pellicle, which is the skin to which the smoke flavor adheres best. (Traditionally, the drying process happens outdoors, in a cool, breezy spot.)

✦ When the fish has dried, stir together the butter and cognac in a small bowl.

✦ Soak the wood chips in a bowl of water for 10 minutes, then drain well.

✦ Prepare your smoker according to the manufacturer's instructions using the damp wood chips, adjusting the heat inside the smoker to between 110 and 150 degrees F (about 125 degrees F is best). Place the fillets on the smoker's grate, baste them with the butter, and smoke them for 30 minutes to 1 hour, depending on the temperature of the smoker and the thickness of your fish, basting again with the butter mixture after the first 20 minutes. The fish is done when it feels firm to the touch and flakes when prodded with a fork on the ends, or when it measures 140 degrees F on an instant-read thermometer in the thickest part of the fillet. (Note that you may need to remove the fillets individually, if they're done at different times.)

✦ When the fish is done, let it come down to room temperature on a cooling rack, then serve. To store the salmon, wrap each fillet individually, first in parchment paper, then in a small zip-top bag, and refrigerate, up to 2 weeks.

strata

button mushrooms, cheddar, leeks, dill

PREP TIME: 45 MINUTES // TOTAL TIME: 24 HOURS // SERVES 12

I REALLY HATE TO ADMIT IT, but I love the smell of sliced white sandwich bread. It reminds me of passing the big white-bread factory near Seattle's International District, where a sugary, yeasty blast of air blankets the neighborhood during baking hours. Perhaps it's because white bread was taboo in my family growing up, or perhaps it's because that sort of bread absorbs egg well. In any case, it's what I always use for strata, the big, messy egg-and-bread dish Italians have made famous. When we did brunch at the original Boat Street Café, we would make one or two strata per day this way, each four or five inches tall, and it would sell out within the first hour or two.

You can cook this in one large pan or divide it between two smaller (roughly eight-by-eight-inch) pans, however you see fit. The smaller pans will only take a bit more than an hour to bake.

NOTE: For variation, feel free to add cooked sausage to the strata or substitute goat cheese for the cheddar.

- ½ cup (1 stick) plus 2 tablespoons unsalted butter, divided
- ¼ cup plus 1 tablespoon extra-virgin olive oil, divided
- 2 pounds button mushrooms, trimmed and halved
- 1 tablespoon kosher salt, plus more to season vegetables
- 3 large leeks, white and light-green parts only, washed well, halved lengthwise, and cut into ½-inch-thick slices (about 4½ cups total)
- 10 large eggs
- 2 tablespoons Dijon mustard
- ½ teaspoon freshly ground black pepper
- 1 teaspoon freshly grated nutmeg
- 1 cup grated Parmesan cheese
- 2 cups whole milk
- 1 cup heavy cream
- 1 cup dry white wine
- 2 (1½-pound) loaves regular sliced organic white bread, each piece cut into thirds
- 2 cups loosely packed chopped fresh dill
- 4 cups grated cheddar cheese (or 1 pound crumbled goat cheese, if you prefer)
- Flaky sea salt, such as Maldon or Jacobsen (see Resources, page 293), for finishing

✦ Start the strata the night before you plan to cook it. First, rub the bottom of a large, deep (13-by-9-inch) baking pan or gratin dish with 2 tablespoons of the butter and set aside. (If using two pans, use 1 tablespoon of butter for each pan.)

continued

+ In a large skillet over medium-high heat, melt 2 tablespoons of the butter with 2 tablespoons of the olive oil. When the butter has melted, add half of the mushrooms, season to taste with kosher salt, and cook, stirring occasionally, until the mushrooms are soft and have given up their water, 3 to 5 minutes. Reduce the heat to low and cook again until the water has evaporated, about 3 more minutes. Transfer the mushrooms to a plate and repeat with another 2 tablespoons of butter, 2 tablespoons olive oil, and the remaining mushrooms. Set aside.

+ Return the pan to medium heat. Add another tablespoon each of butter and olive oil to the pan. When the butter has melted, add the leeks, season to taste with salt, and cook, stirring occasionally, until they are soft and light brown in spots, 8 to 10 minutes. Transfer them to a plate and set aside.

+ In a large metal bowl, whisk the eggs until well blended and foamy. Add the mustard, 1 tablespoon salt, pepper, nutmeg, and Parmesan, and whisk until well blended. Whisk in the milk, cream, and wine, then add the bread. Fold the bread into the egg mixture until almost all of the bread has soaked up the liquid—the bread will fall apart as you mix.

+ Add half of the bread mixture to the baking pan(s). Scatter two-thirds of the mushrooms, leeks, and over the bread, followed by 2 cups of the cheddar. Add the other half of the bread mixture, followed by the remaining mushrooms, leeks, and dill and the remaining 2 cups of cheddar. Dot the top of the strata with the remaining 3 tablespoons butter. Cover the strata with plastic wrap and refrigerate overnight.

+ About two hours before serving, preheat the oven to 350 degrees F. Place the unwrapped strata on a rimmed baking sheet to catch any oil that seeps out during baking.

+ Bake the strata on the oven's middle rack for about 90 minutes, or until the strata is firm and crusty on top, nicely browned, and cooked all the way through. (If the top gets too dark as it bakes, cover it with aluminum foil.) Sprinkle the strata with the sea salt, cover it with foil to keep warm, and let the strata sit for 30 minutes before serving.

spicy pork crépinettes

PREP TIME: 1 HOUR // TOTAL TIME: 12 HOURS // MAKES 24

CRÉPINE IS THE FRENCH WORD FOR caul fat, the thin layer that surrounds a pig's stomach, but I like to think of it as porcine lace. Used here as a package for spicy, harissa-infused sausage, it's sturdy and stretchable, not to mention breathtakingly beautiful. *Crépinettes* are also an easy way to make sausage without stuffing the meat mixture into casings, and because it freezes well (well-wrapped, for up to three months), it's a convenient item to have on hand.

If you grind your own meat for these, make sure everything involved in the grinding process is ice-cold. First, cut the pork shoulder into roughly 1-inch pieces, then freeze the meat on a sheet tray until solid but not yet frozen, about 20 minutes. Freeze all the pieces of your meat grinder as well, rinsing them and freezing them again during the grinding process if the meat becomes difficult to grind.

It's best to make these a day or two in advance; the flavors in the sausage marry over time. Once cooked, the exteriors of the crépinettes have great texture, but not the traditional snap of link sausage.

NOTE: You can grind the spices in a spice grinder, a mortar and pestle, or in the work bowl of a food processor.

---

2 tablespoons whole fennel seeds

2 tablespoons whole cumin seeds

⅓ cup plus 1 tablespoon harissa, such as Rose Petal Harissa (page 282)

2 tablespoons very finely chopped fresh garlic

2 tablespoons red pepper flakes

1 tablespoon ground cinnamon

Grated zest of 1 lemon

Grated zest and juice of 1 lime

1 tablespoon plus 1 teaspoon kosher salt, plus more to season pork

4 pounds cold ground pork shoulder

Olive oil, for frying crépinettes

½ pound caul fat

✦ First, toast the spices: Heat a small skillet over medium heat. When hot, add the fennel and cumin seeds and toast, stirring occasionally, until browned and fragrant, 3 to 4 minutes. Set the spices aside to cool.

✦ In a large mixing bowl, stir together the harissa, garlic, red pepper flakes, cinnamon, lemon zest, lime zest and juice, and 1 tablespoon plus 1 teaspoon kosher salt. Grind the cooled spices and add them to the mixture, then add the pork and mix until thoroughly blended, rubbing it between your fingers to ensure every tiny piece of meat has an even blend of the spices. (This will take a few minutes.)

continued

+ Heat the same skillet over medium heat. When hot, add about a teaspoon of olive oil, then a golf ball–size patty of meat pressed into a disk about ½ inch thick. Cook for 3 to 4 minutes on each side, until cooked through. Let the meat cool and taste it, then adjust the amount of kosher salt in the larger batch accordingly.

+ Portion the pork mixture into 3-ounce disks about ¾ inch thick and 2 inches in diameter and place them on a parchment-lined baking sheet. (You don't need to weigh them, necessarily, but you should end up with 24 patties roughly the size of a crab cake.)

+ On a clean work surface, spread out some of the caul fat (it will likely be in 2 or 3 pieces), trimming off any thick edges. Using a small, sharp knife, cut a roughly 4-inch square out of the caul fat. Place a patty on the square, then wrap the fat around it, stretching and patting until the fat completely covers the patty. Place the patty seam side down on the parchment paper and repeat with the remaining patties and caul fat. (You may need to adjust the size of the crépinette squares based on the size of your patties.) Chill the crépinettes, covered, at least overnight or up to 3 days. (You can also make the crépinettes up to this point, arrange them on waxed paper, and freeze them in zip-top bags for up to 2 months. Thaw them completely in the refrigerator before cooking.)

+ To cook, heat a large, heavy pan over medium heat. When hot, add about 1 tablespoon of oil, then about 6 crépinettes—it's important not to crowd them in the pan. Cook for 6 to 8 minutes per side, or until browned and cooked through. Repeat with the remaining crépinettes. (You shouldn't need to add any more oil, and may want to pour some of the fat out of the pan between batches.) If you'd like, keep the cooked crépinettes warm in a 200-degree oven while you finish the rest. Serve warm.

RUSSELL FLINT, BUTCHER

On a very basic level, finding a butcher you trust—someone you feel comfortable interrogating and who only buys well-raised meat—is a crucial part of cooking. A long time ago, before the advent of plastic wrap, it was how we shopped. Touching, sniffing, and questioning were all part of the meat-buying process; previous generations gossiped with their butcher about whether the rib eye or the T-bone was eating best that week. It's a way of shopping that many people have altogether forgotten.

But in Seattle, Russell Flint, owner of Rain Shadow Meats, is bringing those habits back. At his two Seattle shops, his team sells the best, freshest meat from animals raised by farmers and ranchers he's come to know quite well. He can tell you how to braise a brisket and he'll trim it for you. But most importantly, he can tell you what to cook for dinner.

I met Russell Flint serendipitously, as I have many of the people in my life. He was working as a butcher at Whole Foods, and my mother, a frequent customer of his, informed him that he'd make a great addition to the original Boat Street Café. I hired him, and over time, Russell became an integral part of the restaurant. He started as the sous chef at Boat Street Café when it reopened in 2005, teaching himself to break down whole animals, to make traditional charcuterie, and to cut meat in the traditional French style, so we always had gorgeous bone-in pork chops and perfect pâté. Plus, Russell is quite tall, and in the kitchen he could always reach things for me. Eventually, he decided to open his own shop, so he could provide cuts that aren't commonly available, like the ingredients needed for homemade sausage.

Today, Russell (who I call Fuzzle Flint, because he always wears a fuzzy hat) is one of my crucial links to the industry. He helps me learn what cuts are underappreciated, and he understands what I like, the same way an old-school butcher probably did for my great-grandmother. I ask him what he's taking home—you should always ask butchers what they're eating—and dinner is always delicious.

molasses spice cake

whipped cream, candied orange peel

PREP TIME: 50 MINUTES // TOTAL TIME: 1 HOUR 30 MINUTES // SERVES 10

I LIKE SAVORY FOOD, AND I'M not a baker, which means that when I discover a cake that's filled with curious flavors like mustard, coffee, black pepper, and ginger, and is also simple to bake, I stick with it.

for the CAKE:

2½ cups (about 320 grams) all-purpose flour, sifted, plus more for pan

2 teaspoons baking soda

1½ teaspoons kosher salt

1 tablespoon ground ginger

2 teaspoons ground cinnamon

½ teaspoon dry mustard

½ teaspoon black pepper

½ cup (1 stick) plus 2 tablespoons unsalted butter, softened, plus more for pan

¾ cup sugar

2 large eggs

1 cup molasses

4 shots espresso or ⅔ cup strong brewed coffee, plus whole milk to equal 1 cup, cooled

for the CANDIED ORANGE PEEL:

2 organic Seville or navel oranges

1 cup sugar

2 cups heavy cream, whipped just before serving

✦ Preheat the oven to 325 degrees F. Carefully butter and flour a Bundt pan and set aside.

✦ In a medium bowl, whisk together the flour, baking soda, salt, ginger, cinnamon, mustard, and black pepper to blend.

✦ In the work bowl of a stand mixer fitted with the paddle attachment, cream the butter and sugar together on medium speed for 1 minute, until light. Add the eggs, molasses, and espresso mixture, and mix again on low speed until blended (a few small lumps are okay), scraping down the sides of the bowl with a rubber spatula as needed. Add the dry ingredients, then mix on low speed just until the flour is completely incorporated.

✦ Transfer the batter to the prepared pan and bake for 50 to 60 minutes, or until the cake is puffed and a skewer inserted into the center of the cake comes out squeaky clean. Cool the cake in the pan for 10 minutes, then invert it onto a cooling rack set over a baking sheet and let it cool.

✦ While the cake bakes, make the candied orange peel: First, halve and juice the oranges, then strain the juice into a liquid measuring cup. Carefully cut the pith from the oranges, saving just the orange part of the peel (as for Using Preserved Lemons, see page 13). Slice the peel into ¼-inch-thick strips, transfer them to a small saucepan, and add water to cover. Bring the mixture to a boil, boil the peel for 5 minutes, then drain the water. Add fresh water to the reserved orange juice to make 1 cup of liquid, then add the liquid and the sugar to the pan with the poached orange peel. Return the peel to the heat and cook at a low boil for about 10 minutes, or until the peels are very shiny and almost translucent. Transfer the slices to a piece of parchment paper to dry, and reserve the syrup for glazing the cake.

✦ When the cake has cooled for about 10 minutes, bring the glaze back to a simmer to loosen it up, then brush the glaze all over the top and sides of the cake. Let the glaze soak in for a few minutes, then brush again, repeating until you've used all the glaze.

✦ Serve the cake slightly warm or at room temperature, sliced, with the candied orange peel and freshly whipped cream.

WINTER INGREDIENTS

CARROTS

Raw Carrot Salad with Currants and Walnut Oil

✦ Peel and finely shred **1 pound sweet carrots** and set aside. In a serving bowl, whisk together **1 cup whole milk yogurt**, **½ cup walnut oil**, **½ teaspoon curry powder**, **a pinch of cayenne pepper**, and **⅓ cup currants** softened in hot water. Stir the carrots in and season with **flaky sea salt**. *Serves 4.*

Roasted Baby Carrots with Olive Oil and Thyme

✦ Toss **1 pound baby carrots** (halved if fat) with **2 tablespoons olive oil**, **1 heaping teaspoon fresh thyme leaves**, and **flaky sea salt** to taste. Roast at 450 degrees F for about 15 minutes, until well caramelized. *Serves 4.*

Smooth Carrot and Parsnip Soup

✦ Peel **2 pounds parsnips** and **1 pound carrots**, and chop into bite-size pieces. In a large soup pot, melt **2 tablespoons butter** over medium heat, then add the vegetables and sauté until warm, about 3 minutes. Add enough chicken or vegetable **stock** to cover the vegetables (about 4 cups), bring to a simmer, and cook until the biggest pieces are tender, about 20 minutes. Stir in **¾ cup heavy cream**. Whirl the soup until smooth in a blender, then season with **kosher salt and pepper**. Serve warm or cold. *Serves 4.*

CITRUS

Scallops with Kaffir Lime Salt and Olive Oil

✦ Cut **4 U/10 scallops** into 4 slices across the equator and arrange them on plates. Make kaffir lime salt by mixing **1 tablespoon flaky sea salt** with the **grated zest of 1 kaffir lime**. Sprinkle over the raw scallops to taste, then drizzle each plate with the **juice of a quarter of a lime** and **1 tablespoon of grassy extra-virgin olive oil**. *Serves 4.*

Broiled Grapefruit with Sugar

✦ Top a **grapefruit half** with **1 heaping tablespoon of sugar** (such as the vanilla-scented sugar made with the vanilla bean from the ice cream on page 289) and broil about 3 inches from the top of the oven for just 1 to 2 minutes, until the sugar browns. *Serves 1.*

Lime Curd

✦ Whirl **1½ cups sugar** with the **zest of 5 limes** in a food processor until fine. Melt **1 stick of butter** and the lime sugar together over low heat in a medium saucepan. Add **4 large egg yolks**, whisking them in one at a time, then stir in **½ cup freshly squeezed lime juice** and **¼ teaspoon kosher salt**. Cook over low heat until thick, stirring constantly, about 10 minutes. Remove from the heat, strain, and refrigerate until cool. *Makes 2 cups.*

KALE

Kale Chips with Aleppo Pepper and Sea Salt

✦ Remove the ribs from a **¾-pound bunch lacinato kale**, chop the leaves into bite-size pieces, toss with **3 tablespoons extra-virgin olive oil**, and roast at 350 degrees F for about 25 minutes, or until crisp, stirring once or twice. Transfer to a paper towel–lined plate to drain briefly. Season with **Aleppo pepper** and **flaky sea salt**, and serve immediately. *Serves 4.*

Marinated Kale Salad

✦ Remove ribs from a **¾-pound bunch lacinato or green kale** and chop into bite-size pieces, removing all the tough bits. Dress with **2 tablespoons freshly squeezed lemon juice**, **¼ cup extra-virgin olive oil**, and **kosher salt**, and let sit at room temperature for 1 to 2 hours, or in the refrigerator overnight, until the kale begins to wilt. Serve as is, or with **toasted pine nuts**, **soaked golden raisins**, and **shaved Pecorino Romano cheese**. *Serves 2 to 4.*

Sautéed Kale with Garlic, Lemon Peel, and Olive Oil

✦ Heat a large skillet over medium-high heat. Swirl in **2 tablespoons extra-virgin olive oil**. Add **1 thinly sliced garlic clove**, cook for a few seconds, then add a **½-pound bunch of chopped kale** and the **julienned peel of half a lemon**, and cook until the kale is soft. Squeeze the lemon half's juice over the kale. Stir in **1 tablespoon of butter** and serve hot. *Serves 2 to 4.*

ONIONS

Creamed Caramelized Onion Soup

✦ In a large soup pot, cook **2 pounds sliced onions** over low heat in **¼ cup extra-virgin olive oil** with **3 sprigs fresh thyme**, stirring frequently, for 1 hour or so, until well browned. Add **chicken stock** to cover (about 4 cups), bring to a simmer, and add **½ cup heavy cream**. Cook for 3 minutes, then puree until smooth and season to taste with **kosher salt and pepper**. *Serves 2 to 4.*

Baked Onions with Cream, Olive Oil, Salt, and Pepper

✦ Peel and halve **8 small onions (about 1½ pounds)** horizontally, drizzle with **3 tablespoons extra-virgin olive oil**, season with **kosher salt and pepper**, place in a baking pan, and roast for 45 minutes to 1 hour at 350 degrees F, or until soft and browned, basting once or twice during baking. *Serves 4.*

Onion Agrodolce

✦ Thinly slice **1 pound white onions** with the grain and cook over medium heat in a big pot with **¼ cup olive oil** and **1 bay leaf** until the onion begins to brown, about 20 minutes. Add **½ cup red wine vinegar, 3 tablespoons brown sugar, 1 big sprig fresh thyme, ¼ teaspoon kosher salt,** and **⅛ teaspoon cayenne pepper** and cook another 10 minutes, until the sugar is incorporated and the onions are well caramelized but before the mixture begins to burn. Remove the bay leaf, then serve the *agrodolce* with sausages or chicken. *Makes about 2 cups.*

POTATOES

Potato Leek Soup

✦ Clean and thinly slice **2 fat leeks (about 1½ pounds)**. In a large pot, melt **½ stick unsalted butter** over medium heat, then add the leeks and cook until very soft but not browned, about 15 minutes. Add **6 fist-size peeled and quartered white potatoes (about 3 pounds)**, then add **chicken stock** to cover (about 6 cups). Bring the soup to a simmer, then cook until the potatoes are totally soft, about 20 minutes. Blend the soup, thin with stock if needed, then season with **kosher salt and a pinch of cayenne pepper**. You can serve the soup warm or cold; just be sure to season it at the temperature at which you're going to serve it. *Serves 6 to 8.*

Potato Pavés with Roasted Chicken

✦ In a well-buttered 8-inch (or similar) gratin dish, arrange **8 peeled and very thinly sliced fist-size white potatoes (about 2 pounds)** in layers until they reach the top, drizzling **2 tablespoons melted butter** over the potatoes and seasoning them with **flaky sea salt and pepper** at least 3 times as you layer them. (It's easiest to slice the potatoes on a mandoline; aim for about ⅛-inch thick.) Dot the potatoes with **1 additional tablespoon butter**. Drizzle **½ cup cream** over the dish and bake at 375 degrees F for 45 minutes to 1 hour, until crisp and tanned on top and tender in the center. Let the *pavés* rest for about 15 minutes, then cut into squares and serve with roasted chicken (see recipe for Roasted Chicken, page 257). *Serves 6 to 8.*

Smashed Potato and Carrot Gratin

✦ Boil **8 fist-size Yukon Gold potatoes (about 2 pounds)** and **8 large peeled carrots (about 1 pound)** separately in salted water until tender, then drain. In the work bowl of a stand mixer fitted with the paddle attachment, whip the potatoes and carrots together until partially mashed. Transfer to a gratin dish, season with **kosher salt and pepper**, and top with **¾ cup heavy cream**. Bake at 350 degrees F for 45 minutes to 1 hour, until bubbly and crisp on the top. *Serves 8.*

A Holiday Supper

Pickled Mussel Toasts *45*
Garlic Aioli

Gougères *47*
Gruyère, Piment d'Espelette

Standing Rib Roast *49*
Horseradish Cream

Lacinato Kale Gratin *52*

Celery Root and Celery Leaf Salad *56*
Poppy Seeds, Walnuts,
Meyer Lemon Vinaigrette

Boat Street Bread Pudding *59*
Raisins, Orange Peel,
Bourbon Sauce, Cream

SERVES 6 TO 8

IT SEEMS THAT NO MATTER WHAT I DO, there's a certain amount of chaos involved in hosting a dinner party. Ultimately, though, the chaos is part of what I love. I think it's fun to create a beautiful space for people to eat in. I love the flowers and the tablecloth and the silverware I dragged home from Europe. And more than anything, I love eating in my own home, because I do it so seldom. The dishes and the crystal are conduits, too, leading me back to memories about traveling with people I love.

Well before I start planning for a menu, making shopping lists and such, I go through my home and figure out what I need. I dump old things out of my freezer, find out whether I have enough sugar, and generally get my house in order before I start destroying and then rebeautifying my kitchen. Even with a menu that comes together relatively easily, like this English-inspired one, I start thinking about dinner at least a week in advance.

Over the holidays, I look forward to what I consider to be the perfect traditional dinner party, which means a gathering with about eight people and plenty of wine and food. (With parties larger than eight, I think the cook often ends up feeling like the help.) I lean toward old-fashioned food, simply because the classics exist for a reason; they're warming and comforting and dependably delicious. I also lean toward inviting people into my kitchen as the food cooks, because part of the art of throwing a party is about allowing other people to help and participate. I choose the dishes, but I let others help me set the table. It's about preparing well and then letting go of perfection.

When I say this menu serves six to eight, I mean you can serve big portions to six people, like I do, and still have plenty to nibble on the next day.

pickled mussel toasts

garlic aioli

PREP TIME: 45 MINUTES // TOTAL TIME: 45 MINUTES, PLUS PICKLING TIME
MAKES ABOUT 2 DOZEN

STEAMED AND PICKLED, TENDER PUGET SOUND mussels make a great toast topping. We get our mussels from Hood Canal, a deep, cold body of water about two hours southwest of Seattle. They're delicious because they're happy mussels; Hood Canal provides each bivalve with enough nutrition to plump up beautifully. Since mussels' size varies, decide how many to place atop each toast based on their bulk; use three if the mussels are small, or just two if they're larger.

You can also serve the cooked mussels (before pickling) hot for dinner, with an extra dab of butter and Grilled Bread (page 277) for mopping up the juices.

for the MUSSELS:
2 tablespoons unsalted butter
1 garlic clove, thinly sliced
1 shallot, thinly sliced
2 cups dry white wine
1 big sprig fresh thyme
1 dried arból chili
½ teaspoon kosher salt
¼ teaspoon coriander seeds (fresh,
   if you can find them)
2 pounds mussels, cleaned and
   debearded
2 tablespoons extra-virgin olive oil

for the PICKLING LIQUID:
3 tablespoons extra-virgin olive oil
2 garlic cloves, thinly sliced
2 shallots, thinly sliced
2 cups white wine vinegar
3 dried arból chilis
1 teaspoon fennel seed
1 teaspoon kosher salt

2 dozen Baguette Toasts
   (page 278)
1 cup Garlic Aioli (page 281)

✦ In a large soup pot with a lid, melt the butter over medium heat. Add the garlic and shallot and cook, stirring, for 3 minutes, or until the shallots are soft. Add the wine, thyme, chili, salt, and coriander, bring to a simmer, and cook for 1 minute. Add the mussels and steam, covered, for 2 to 3 minutes. Open the lid and, using tongs, transfer the opened mussels to a large bowl. Continue cooking, transferring mussels as they open, until all the mussels have opened. (Discard any that do not open.) Set the cooked mussels aside.

✦ In a saucepan, make the pickling liquid: Heat the olive oil over medium heat. Add the garlic and shallots and cook, stirring occasionally, for 3 minutes, or until both are soft. Add the vinegar, chilis, fennel, and salt, and simmer for 4 minutes. Remove the liquid from the heat and let cool for about 10 minutes.

continued

+ Meanwhile, pick the mussels from their shells and transfer them to a bowl or large jar. Pour the pickling liquid over the mussels, cover, and refrigerate for at least 2 hours, or up to 24 hours.

+ Let the mussels come to room temperature in their liquid about 2 hours before serving. To serve, drain the mussels (reserve the shallots and other pickling bits), then toss the mussels and pickled shallots with the olive oil. (You'll use the mussels and the shallots separately, but it's fine if they're all mixed together here.)

+ Smear each toast with about 2 teaspoons of the aioli. Top each toast with 2 to 3 mussels (depending on their size), garnish with some of the pickled shallots (with any garlic and fennel mixed in), and serve immediately.

gougères

gruyère, piment d'espelette

PREP TIME: 35 MINUTES // TOTAL TIME: 1 HOUR 40 MINUTES
MAKES ABOUT 2 DOZEN

MY FRIEND ROBERT PETERSON HAS A *gougère* addiction. I make them every year for his birthday dinner, itself an odd collection of foods also including, but not limited to, potato salad with a stack of naked cooked bacon piled on top. But getting birthday gougères is never enough. Once, I filled a grocery bag for an opening at Curtis Steiner's art store. The entire bag disappeared; Robert just never got around to putting them out with the rest of the appetizers. Should your tastes run the same way his do, feel free to eat them all in the privacy of your own bedroom and substitute another bite for these pretty puffs, such as Herring Butter Toasts (page 68). Otherwise, serve them with dinner, and encourage guests to use them to mop up the juices from the Standing Rib Roast (page 49)—think Yorkshire pudding with a French accent.

Ages ago, I learned to make gougères from Julia Child's *Mastering the Art of French Cooking*. Today, my recipe is still based on hers, but I always add *piment d'Espelette* (see Resources, page 293), for a hint of spice and a lovely orange color. Make them just before the party, if you can, or make them earlier in the day and recrisp them for a few minutes in a 400-degree oven before serving.

½ cup (1 stick) unsalted butter
1½ cups whole milk
1 tablespoon kosher salt
½ teaspoon piment d'Espelette (or
   1 teaspoon if you enjoy spice)
¼ teaspoon freshly grated nutmeg
1½ cups (about 192 grams)
   all-purpose flour, sifted

5 large eggs, at room temperature
1 cup grated Gruyère cheese
½ cup finely grated Parmesan
   cheese
Flaky sea salt, such as Maldon or
   Jacobsen (see Resources, page
   293), for finishing

✦ In a large saucepan, heat the butter, milk, salt, piment d'Espelette, and nutmeg together over low heat until the butter has melted completely. Add the flour, stirring vigorously until the mixture forms a paste, then cook, stirring and smearing the dough constantly, until the mixture starts to smell nutty and small beads of fat form on the surface of the dough that's just come off the bottom of the pan, about 10 minutes total. (I usually stop stirring when my arm hurts too much to continue. It will be thick, like sugar cookie dough.)

✦ Transfer the dough to the work bowl of a stand mixer fitted with the paddle attachment and let cool for 15 minutes, or until the dough has almost reached room temperature. Preheat the oven to 425 degrees F. Line two baking sheets with parchment paper and set them aside.

continued

✦ When the dough has cooled, with the machine on medium speed, add the eggs one at a time, mixing until the batter reforms between each egg and scraping down the sides of the bowl as necessary. When you have added all the eggs, mix in the Gruyère and Parmesan on low speed.

✦ Using two spoons, form the batter into golf ball–size balls and arrange them on the prepared baking sheets about 1½ inches apart, dipping the spoons into a bowl of warm water between each one. Sprinkle the gougères liberally with the sea salt.

✦ Bake the gougères for 10 minutes. Without opening the oven door, reduce the temperature to 350 degrees F and bake for another 25 minutes, or until the gougères are brown and crisp on the outside and half hollow in the center.

✦ Serve immediately, or let cool on cooling racks and serve within a few hours.

standing rib roast

horseradish cream

PREP TIME: 25 MINUTES // TOTAL TIME: 1 HOUR 30 MINUTES, PLUS RESTING TIME
SERVES 6 TO 8

THEY CALL IT A STANDING RIB roast for a reason; cut from a cow's center ribs, this outsized cut of beef has clean-scraped ribs that traditionally roast standing straight up. If you ask your butcher to "French and trim" one for roasting, he'll use the back of a knife to remove all the fat and cartilage from around each bone. He'll also remove the silver skin and hard fat from the top of the roast, but he shouldn't remove the soft fat; this is what will melt into the meat and give it its signature unctuous flavor.

Remember that the roast will continue to cook after you remove it from the oven; it's crucial to give the meat some rest and relaxation before serving it with the Lacinato Kale Gratin (page 52).

NOTE: Cows are all different sizes. We buy our meat from a rancher who doesn't use a feed lot, so the cows do tend to be smaller. Six pounds should be plenty for a crowd, but the number of ribs will depend on the cow those ribs come from.

---

1 (4-rib) standing rib roast, about
 6 to 7 pounds total, Frenched
 and trimmed
5 tablespoons extra-virgin olive oil,
 divided

3 tablespoons crushed flaky sea
 salt, such as Maldon or Jacobsen
 (see Resources, page 293)
Horseradish Cream, for serving
 (recipe follows)

✦ Allow the meat to rest at room temperature for about 30 minutes before roasting.

✦ Preheat the oven to 400 degrees F.

✦ On the stove, heat a large, heavy skillet over medium heat. While the pan heats, drizzle the roast with 3 tablespoons of the olive oil, using your hands to rub it all over the roast, then sprinkle the salt over all sides, patting it in to encourage it to stick. (It's okay if some falls off.) Add the remaining 2 tablespoons of oil to the pan, then sear the roast on all sides until deep golden brown, turning the meat occasionally—only when it lifts easily from the pan without sticking—about 15 minutes total.

continued

+ Transfer the meat to a roasting pan and roast, basting every 15 minutes or so, until the meat registers 125 to 130 degrees F on an instant-read thermometer inserted into the thickest part of the roast, 50 minutes to 1 hour. Cover the meat with a tent of aluminum foil and let it rest at room temperature for 30 minutes.

+ To serve, remove the string, if used, and cut the meat into ½-inch slices. Serve on a large platter, with the Horseradish Cream alongside.

horseradish cream

PREP TIME: 10 MINUTES // TOTAL TIME: 10 MINUTES // MAKES 2 CUPS

FRESH HORSERADISH IS VASTLY UNDERUSED; I love it on steak and oysters, or as a substitute for garlic in gremolata. Stirred into a simple mixture of sour cream and cream, it makes an excellent sauce for any cut of beef.

You can make this up to three hours ahead and store it in the refrigerator until the roast goes in, but horseradish turns cream gray over time, so don't make it the day before.

NOTE: Once it's peeled, keep fresh horseradish fresher longer by storing it in the refrigerator, submerged in a glass of water.

---

1 cup sour cream
1 loosely packed cup finely grated
   fresh horseradish
½ cup heavy cream
Juice of half a medium lemon

1 teaspoon flaky sea salt, such
   as Maldon or Jacobsen (see
   Resources, page 293), for
   finishing

+ In a small bowl, whisk together the sour cream, horseradish, heavy cream, lemon juice, and sea salt until well blended. Season to taste with additional salt, then refrigerate, covered, until about an hour or so before serving. Serve the sauce at room temperature.

lacinato kale gratin

PILED HIGH INTO A GRATIN DISH raw and layered with sharp cheddar cheese, lacinato kale makes a most heavenly gratin—the leaves on the edges get fluttery and crisp, while the center turns to a melting pot of kale, cream, and cheese. It's perfect winter food, if you ask me.

If you'd like to make this a bit ahead of time, bake it as directed and let it cool to room temperature a few hours before dinner. Before serving, top the gratin with about ½ cup additional grated sharp cheddar cheese and reheat the gratin in a 350-degree oven for about 10 minutes, until it is bubbling again.

NOTE: It's important to get the tough center ribs out of each kale leaf. I hold the fat end of the stem in one hand, and pull down toward the tip of each leaf with the other hand, stripping the greens off as I go.

---

3 bunches lacinato kale (about 1½ pounds total before trimming), tough ribs removed, chopped into 3-inch sections
½ teaspoon freshly grated nutmeg
Kosher salt and freshly ground black pepper

3 cups heavy cream
8 ounces sharp white cheddar cheese, such as Beecher's Flagship (see Resources, page 293), cut into ⅛-inch-thick slices

→ Preheat the oven to 350 degrees F.

→ Pile the kale in a 9-by-13-inch (or similar) baking dish. (It will seem like an overabundance of kale, towering above the pan's edge, but you want it all.) Season the kale with the nutmeg and salt and pepper to taste, then carefully drizzle the cream over it. Spread out the cheese slices over the kale.

→ Place the gratin dish on a baking sheet to catch any cream that drips out as the gratin cooks. Bake the gratin for 50 minutes to 1 hour, or until the cream thickens and the cheese is nicely browned. (Err on the side of golden brown, as opposed to coffee brown, if you're going to reheat the gratin again before serving.)

→ Let the gratin cool for a few minutes, then serve.

CURTIS STEINER, AESTHETE

Curtis Steiner claims to be the oldest living Boat Street Café customer. I highly doubt that's true, but I do know he's its most influential one—according to me, at least. In 1997, then-owner Susan Kaplan hired Curtis to do a chalkboard sketch. I remember calling her to make sure she knew a man was drawing Chihuahuas on her wall. Back then, he'd often come in for dinner, and we started chatting. Today, he's one of my best friends.

As befits the owner of an eponymous jewelry, furniture, and card shop in Seattle's Ballard neighborhood, Curtis's home is, in a word, interesting. (It even has a literal secret garden, accessible only to those who are told exactly where to go.) Tucked behind another house in a quiet Seattle neighborhood, past an ancient, gnarly cherry tree, is a smallish house that Curtis treats more or less like a museum. The walls are covered—quite literally—with drawings, objects, and ephemera, and he's constantly curating new corners and collecting quirky things, from ugly antique bulldog figurines to rice-steaming balls.

His continuous and energetic revamping has taught me that decor is an evolving thing at my restaurants. At Boat Street Café, for example, when he threw a party for his partner, Robert Peterson, he decorated the ceiling with giant paper umbrellas (see page 3) for a whimsical, summery effect. I asked him if I could keep them, and they've since become one of the hallmarks of the space. Today, in part because of him, I'm constantly on the lookout for items to add to my dining rooms.

Curtis is also a self-described despot; he likes what he likes even if it means taking risks with color, texture, and style. Because of him, I've learned to stick to my instincts when it comes to decorating, and to care about every single detail. I think it's helped my restaurants' success.

When Curtis throws parties—holiday parties, usually—his space morphs into a magical, sparkly spot, with lights glimmering from what must be the most intricately decorated holiday tree on the planet. This menu was designed for a party at his beautiful house.

celery root and celery leaf salad
poppy seeds, walnuts, meyer lemon vinaigrette

PREP TIME: 45 MINUTES // TOTAL TIME: 45 MINUTES // SERVES 6 TO 8

ONCE YOU GET PAST ITS INTIMIDATING appearance, celery root is lovely, with a delicious, green vegetal flavor that's hard to come by in the dead of winter. It's also not sweet like most winter vegetables, which I love.

Peel celery root with a vegetable peeler, digging out any knots in the root with a knife, or trim especially gnarly specimens with a small knife. To shave it, use a mandoline (see My Favorite Tools, page 14) or cut it as thinly as possible with a large, sharp knife.

Use preserved Meyer lemons if you can find them or make them (follow the recipe for Preserved Lemons on page 211, but substitute Meyer lemons for the regular kind); otherwise, use regular store-bought preserved lemons (see Resources, page 293). Also, if your celery doesn't have much in the way of internal leaves, substitute fresh Italian parsley.

for the VINAIGRETTE:
Julienned peel of 2 preserved
  Meyer lemons (see Using
  Preserved Lemons, page 13)
1 scant cup crème fraîche
2 tablespoons freshly squeezed
  lemon juice (from 1 medium
  lemon)
1 teaspoon minced shallot
1 cup extra-virgin olive oil
1 tablespoon plus 1 teaspoon
  poppy seeds
Kosher salt

for the SALAD:
3 baseball-size celery roots (about
  2 pounds total), well peeled
1 cup whole walnuts, toasted (see
  Toasting Nuts, page 12), divided
1 cup picked celery leaves (from
  the heart of regular celery)
2 teaspoons poppy seeds
¾ cup pomegranate seeds
Extra-virgin olive oil (see
  Resources, page 293), for
  drizzling
Flaky sea salt, such as Maldon or
  Jacobsen (see Resources, page
  293), for finishing

✦ First, make the vinaigrette: In the work bowl of a food processor or a heavy-duty blender, whirl the preserved lemon peel, crème fraîche, lemon juice, and shallot until the lemon peel is finely chopped. With the motor running, add the olive oil in a slow, steady stream through the top of the machine, processing until smooth and creamy. Season to taste with kosher salt. (Some preserved lemons are saltier than others, so use your judgment.) Transfer the dressing to a large bowl.

✦ Make the salad: Using a mandoline or a large, sharp knife, shave the celery root into ⅛-inch-thick slices, adding the root to the bowl with the dressing as you slice it to prevent it from turning brown. Separate the celery root and make sure you get dressing on each piece. When all the celery root has been mixed in, stir in about three-quarters of the walnuts, crushing them a bit in your hands as you add them to the bowl. (You can store the celery root, without the walnuts, in the refrigerator for up to 4 hours after mixing it with the dressing. Bring it to room temperature before serving.)

✦ Transfer the mixture to a large platter, then garnish with the remaining walnuts, celery leaves, poppy seeds, and pomegranate seeds. Serve at room temperature, drizzled with extra-virgin olive oil and showered with sea salt.

boat street bread pudding

raisins, orange peel, bourbon sauce, cream

PREP TIME: 35 MINUTES // TOTAL TIME: 1 HOUR 35 MINUTES,
PLUS TIME TO SOAK RAISINS // SERVES 6 TO 8

WITHOUT THE OPPORTUNITIES SUSAN KAPLAN GAVE me when I worked for her
at the original Boat Street Café, I might have been peeling onions for another
four years before being given the chance to really cook, and for that, I am eternally grateful. I'm also grateful that she introduced me to the ancestor of the
bread pudding now served at the current Boat Street, which is a perennial guest
favorite. In this version, I bake the pudding the morning I plan to serve it in a
giant baking dish, then slice it, douse it with a bourbon-based butter sauce, and
bake it again just before serving.

It's okay to use day-old bread for this recipe, but anything older will make the
pudding dry and a bit crumbly.

for the BREAD PUDDING:
1 cup golden raisins
½ cup bourbon, such as Buffalo
   Trace
3 large eggs
1½ cups sugar
Grated zest of 1 large orange
1 teaspoon vanilla extract
½ teaspoon kosher salt
4 cups heavy cream
1 large baguette (about 1 pound),
   torn into 1-inch pieces

for the SAUCE:
½ cup (1 stick) unsalted butter
2 cups confectioners' sugar, sifted
¾ cup bourbon, such as Buffalo
   Trace
Pinch of kosher salt
1 (14-ounce) can sweetened
   condensed milk

2 cups heavy cream, for serving

✦ First, soak the raisins: In a small bowl, combine the raisins and bourbon, cover,
and let sit at room temperature for at least 1 hour, or up to 1 day. Drain the raisins and set them aside, reserving the bourbon for the sauce.

✦ Preheat the oven to 350 degrees F.

✦ Make the bread pudding: In a large mixing bowl, whisk together the eggs,
sugar, orange zest, vanilla, and ½ teaspoon kosher salt until blended. Add the
cream, whisk to blend, then add the bread pieces and raisins, stirring the mixture
together with a large spoon until every piece of bread is coated in the pudding.
Transfer the mixture to a 9-by-13-inch (or similar) baking pan.

continued

✦ Place the baking dish on a baking sheet to catch any drips, and bake on the middle rack of the oven for about 1 hour, or until the top layer of bread is nicely browned, the edges are bubbling, and the center of the pudding is firm to the touch. Remove the bread pudding from the oven and let cool. Turn the oven off. (I typically make the pudding up to this point and let it cool completely before continuing, but it's okay to serve it right away.)

✦ Make the sauce: In a small saucepan, melt the butter over low heat. Whisk in the confectioners' sugar until it has melted into the butter completely. Next, carefully add the reserved bourbon and the ¾ cup bourbon, and bring the sauce to a strong simmer. Cook the mixture for 6 to 8 minutes, until all the alcohol has burned off. (You can also light the mixture on fire, if you're the dramatic type, and wait for the fire to die.) Add the salt, whisk in the condensed milk, and continue to stir and thicken the sauce for another minute or two. Set the sauce aside to cool until ready to serve. (If you'd like, you can refrigerate the sauce for up to 3 days before serving.)

✦ To serve, preheat the oven again, to 400 degrees F. Scoop the bread pudding into large, shallow ovenproof bowls and drizzle with about ¼ cup of the sauce. Carefully slide the bowls into the oven and bake for about 5 minutes, or until the sauce is bubbly, then serve immediately, topped with an indecent amount of cream. (Don't be stingy; each serving should have about ¼ cup heavy cream on top of the sauce.)

BUYING WINE FOR THE HOLIDAYS

How much wine?
Every time you throw a party, there's the inevitable pause when you're trying to decide how much wine to bring home. I don't think I'm a good example of knowing how to order the right amount of wine, because the restaurant crowd probably drinks a lot more than most. I'm also not a big cocktail fan, so I assume wine drinking begins the minute folks walk through the door, not when dinner starts. That said, people generally drink three to four glasses of wine over the course of an evening. I figure on a bottle per person, or sometimes more, because there's typically someone who shows up unexpectedly.

Which wines?
If there are ten people at a party, I usually pick three or four different wines—usually a sparkling, two whites, and one red, because I tend to prefer white. I also buy wine differently depending on who is coming to dinner. However, I think there's an opportunity to learn things when

someone serves you an unfamiliar wine—so, frankly, choose the wine combination that makes you happy.

Buy your wine from a wine shop or a grocery store where you can speak to the wine buyer directly, or to someone who can tell you a bit about each bottle. It's frustrating to spend $15 or $50 on a bottle of wine and not like it, so if you can develop a relationship with a good wine person, you can go back and tell them what you liked or didn't like about it, and they can help choreograph your choices for the next time. As much as you'd use a butcher to buy meat from someone who knows it well, buy your wine from someone who knows the wine.

What I like

I like French wines because they're diverse and extremely site-specific. French pours are also extremely easy to pair with food if you know French cuisine because the terroir of the grapes used almost always matches the food of the region. For example, the sauvignon blancs of the Loire Valley, an appellation that follows the Loire River to the Atlantic Ocean, are best with simple dishes, oysters, and acidic goat cheeses—all food indigenous to the area.

MY FAVORITE HOLIDAY WINES

Champagne

+ Pierre Péters, "Cuvée de Réserve" Brut Blanc de Blancs

+ François Chidaine, Montlouis Méthode Traditionnelle Sparkling Brut NV

Côtes du Rhône

+ Domaine Gramenon, La Sagesse

Morgon

+ Marcel Lapierre

Muscadet

+ Domaine de la Pepiere, "Clos de Briords"

Pear Cider

+ Eric Bordelet, Poiré Granit

New Year's Eve Party

Zetter Martini *65*
Anchovy-Stuffed Olive, Preserved Lemon

Steak Tartare *67*
Rye Toasts or Duck Fat–Fried Potatoes

Herring Butter Toasts *68*
Pickled Fennel, Lemon Peel, Parsley

Boquerones Toasts *73*
Butter, Fresh Horseradish, Ikura

Boat Street Chicken Liver Pâté *74*
Pickled Shallots

Seared Scallops *76*
Crème Fraîche, Herring Roe, Dill

Gâteau de Crêpes *78*
Marmalade, Whipped Cream

SERVES 1 2

As a chef and restaurant owner, I have a big bouquet of responsibilities. With my stellar staff, I run a handful of restaurants, hopefully well. I want to make the food and the places pretty. I want to make people happy. But the more my restaurants grow, the more I realize that, like many chefs, I have the opportunity to help redefine diners' tastes and direct how we source our food. I spend a lot of my time learning about food.

Today, that means thinking hard about where my products come from. Since I have access to well-raised beef, beautiful produce, and gorgeous, sustainably caught seafood near Seattle, I have the luxury of ordering the best of each. But more importantly, perhaps, I have a handful of excellent purveyors who constantly offer me new things to try. If Warner Lew, the Western Alaska fleet manager for Seattle-based Icicle Seafoods, hands me a piece of kelp snowy with fresh-laid herring roe as we cruise the herring-stocked waters of Alaska, I'll taste it. And soon, so will you.

When the New Year rolls around, I celebrate, but perhaps not in the usual way. It's less about resolution, more about revolution. I make food I don't have to spend a lot of time cooking at the last minute, and it's always in small-bite form, so guests can pick and snack all night. The flavors are decadent and intense—celebratory, because they should be—but the portions are never large. Every year, I think about what I've learned and tasted in the previous year, so the flavors are often a reflection of the evolution of my own taste. And there's always something new.

zetter martini

anchovy-stuffed olive, preserved lemon

PREP TIME: 5 MINUTES // TOTAL TIME: 5 MINUTES // MAKES 1

A FEW STEPS FROM THE FAMED Zetter Hotel in London's Clerkenwell neighborhood is the Zetter Townhouse, a quirky Georgian inn with a foyer cocktail bar that's part antiques museum, part library, and wacky from top to bottom. It's the only place I've ever seen a taxidermied cat gussied up in a blue frock, and perhaps the only place that serves icy vermouth- and sherry-tinged martinis in bulbous little cups with a pot of fried olives. When I visited the Townhouse with Curtis Steiner, we knew instantly that the recipe needed to come home with us.

This is my kind of martini—and honestly, there aren't many—but I have a weak spot for both sherry and vermouth. I also like a very cold, fresh martini; I think that's best achieved mixing each drink individually, so this recipe makes just one. Multiply it to match your crowd (and its drinking habits).

For tips on where to source the products below, see Resources (page 293).

2½ ounces gin, such as Voyager, Bombay Sapphire, or Big Gin; or vodka, such as Stoli
½ ounce Dolin dry vermouth
¼ ounce Manzanilla sherry

1 anchovy-stuffed olive
1 (2-by-½-inch) strip preserved lemon peel (see Using Preserved Lemons, page 13)

✦ Fill a cocktail shaker with ice. Add the gin, vermouth, and sherry, and stir well with a long spoon. Strain into a chilled martini glass. Garnish with the olive and lemon peel.

ON VERMOUTH

Vermouth is a fortified wine, native to Italy, that you'll find in many of the most classic cocktails, such as martinis, Manhattans, and Negronis. Today, there are myriad varieties available, which are differentiated by the aromatics and botanicals each producer uses, and by the amounts of alcohol and sugar added to them. In general, vermouth is typically divided into two categories, dry and sweet, with the former typically lighter in color. I'm partial to French-made Dolin Vermouth de Chambéry, which is light and relatively dry. To me, it adds the perfect amount of sweetness to a drink. Our bar manager at The Whale Wins, Michael Getz, makes a perfect vermouth cocktail by blending equal parts white vermouth—an increasingly popular third type—and dry vermouth, and garnishing it with orange peel.

steak tartare

rye toasts or duck fat–fried potatoes

PREP TIME: 30 MINUTES // TOTAL TIME: 30 MINUTES
SERVES 12 AT A PARTY, OR 6 AS A SHARED SIT-DOWN APPETIZER

TARTARE IS A PERENNIAL FAVORITE AT The Walrus and the Carpenter, where we make it with great New York steak, as here, or with lamb. I love serving this with rye toast as an appetizer, but if you're serving it as a main course, accompany it with duck fat–fried potatoes. Either way, you'll need to instruct newbies to break the yolk as they dig in, mixing a bit of it with each meaty bite.

Since you'll be eating the yolks raw, use the best eggs you can find. (Ditto for the meat.) Note that while you can prepare the meat mixture an hour or two ahead and refrigerate it, with a layer of plastic wrap pressed directly onto the meat's surface, it's crucial to add the egg yolks right before serving. For a party, I often separate the tartare onto three small plates and set just one out at a time, cracking a new yolk on top each time I refresh the plate.

½ cup extra-virgin olive oil
¼ cup capers (salt-packed preferred), rinsed well and finely chopped (see Capers, page 188)
¼ cup finely chopped shallot
2 tablespoons finely chopped cornichons
Grated zest of 1 lemon
1½ tablespoons freshly squeezed lemon juice, or to taste (from 1 medium lemon)

2 teaspoons flaky sea salt, such as Maldon or Jacobsen (see Resources, page 293), plus more for finishing
12 ounces New York steak, trimmed of fat and finely chopped
¼ cup minced fresh chives
3 organic eggs (any size)
Finishing oil, for drizzling
2 dozen Rye Toasts (page 278) or Duck Fat–Fried Potatoes (page 279), for serving

✦ In a medium bowl, stir together the olive oil, capers, shallot, cornichons, lemon zest and juice, and 2 teaspoons salt, crushing the salt with your fingers as you add it to the bowl. Add the steak, mixing and mashing until well blended. Taste for seasoning, adding more salt and/or lemon juice if necessary, then gently stir in the chives.

✦ To serve, form the meat into three football-shaped mounds (called quenelles) on one or more platters. Using the pointy end of an egg, make an indentation in the top of each mound. Crack the eggs one at a time, discarding the white and carefully setting each yolk into the center of one mound. Garnish the yolks with sea salt, drizzle the meat and egg with olive oil, and serve immediately, with rye toasts or duck fat–fried potatoes.

herring butter toasts

pickled fennel, lemon peel, parsley

PREP TIME: 15 MINUTES // TOTAL TIME: 15 MINUTES, PLUS TIME
TO TOAST BAGUETTE // MAKES 24

IF HERRING BUTTER SOUNDS STRANGE TO you, think of it as rillettes made with rich, smoked fish instead of the typical pork—it's flavorful, creamy, addictive, and equally friendly to a picklish topping. Note that this butter can be made with any soft canned fish; smoked sardines make an excellent substitution. However, if you're using smoked salmon, use six ounces instead of the four called for here, because the flavor isn't quite as strong as herring or sardines.

4 ounces oil-packed, smoked herring or sardines, oil drained (see
Resources, page 293)
1 cup (2 sticks) unsalted butter,
softened
1 tablespoon finely chopped
shallot
½ teaspoon Dijon mustard
Pinch of cayenne pepper
Crushed flaky sea salt, such
as Maldon or Jacobsen (see

Resources, page 293), for
finishing
1 cup Pickled Fennel (page 213),
liquid drained
1 tablespoon extra-virgin olive oil
2 dozen Baguette Toasts
(page 278)
Finely julienned peel of 1 large
lemon
¼ cup loosely packed fresh Italian
parsley leaves, thinly sliced
(chiffonade), for serving

✦ In the work bowl of a stand mixer fitted with the paddle attachment, whip the fish, butter, shallot, mustard, and cayenne on high speed for a minute or two, until the mixture is homogenous, scraping down the sides of the bowl with a spatula if needed. Taste the butter, then season to taste with salt, and mix again. (Different fish have different saltiness levels, so it's important to taste before salting.) Transfer the mixture to a bowl. (You can make the butter up to this point and refrigerate, covered, until ready to use, up to one week, but it won't be as fluffy as if you make it immediately before serving. Let the mixture come to room temperature for about 4 hours before spreading. If the butter still seems a bit too firm to spread, work it on a clean cutting board with a pastry scraper, or don latex gloves and knead it with your hands until soft.)

✦ Before serving, in a small bowl, stir together the pickled fennel and the olive oil. Set aside.

✦ To serve, spread each of the toasts with about a tablespoon of the herring butter. Top with a chubby pile of pickled fennel, a few strips of lemon peel, and a pinch of parsley.

WARNER LEW, HERRING FISHERMAN

In Seattle, as in a few American cities, there is a herring cult. Scandinavia and Japan might say we're centuries behind, but in the United States, herring and other little oily fish are only now getting their due. At The Walrus and the Carpenter, where the menu focuses on sustainably caught shellfish and less common fish, you'll often find fried smelts, anchovy toasts, or pickled sardines—all homages to the kind of fish that, like herring, bring big, bold flavors. But few restaurants are actually serving herring *fish*, as opposed to herring *roe*.

The herring industry isn't much like other fisheries. It's difficult first because its primary objective is to harvest the delicate roe (almost all herring is caught to satisfy the Japanese market for *kazunoko*, so that delicious carcass is actually considered a by-product) and second because the catch process often takes place in the span of just ten days.

To the untrained eye, herring fishing is total bedlam. When the run starts, the herring move shoreward in glittering schools thick enough to be seen from the air. From a seat next to the pilot, you can trace their path by following the predatory trail of hungry birds and sea lions that follow them.

There are literally hundreds of boats, from small herring-transporting tenders to medium seiners to huge processing vessels. Each company's seiner is connected by radio to its sister ships and the aircraft above, and every part of every machine seems to be moving. The planes guide the fishing vessels as they lay giant nets to surround the herring, but multiple fishing operations are all going after the same schools, creating a fast, intricately choreographed marine rodeo.

Once the fish are caught, they're taken to processing plants overseas where the roe is removed, and mostly sent to Japan. A small portion of the carcasses is sold as bait. And an even tinier portion of the fish—usually less than 1,000 pounds—is sent, whole, to a little restaurant in Seattle.

I salute herring fishermen like Warner Lew because his fish are fantastic, but also because of what he represents to me: a slow, sure movement toward eating parts of the food chain we've ignored, and a willingness to be open to new possibilities.

boquerones toasts

butter, fresh horseradish, ikura

PREP TIME: 15 MINUTES // TOTAL TIME: 15 MINUTES, PLUS TIME TO MAKE
TOASTS // MAKES 24

WHILE MOST AMERICAN OR ITALIAN FLAT-PACKED anchovies are simply cooked
and packed in oil, *boquerones*, Spanish white anchovies, are usually vinegar-
pickled before their olive oil bath. They have a mild, tangy flavor and a fluffier
texture than regular anchovies. Laid out on a bed of butter and topped with
freshly grated horseradish and a pile of *ikura*, or salmon roe, they make an excellent appetizer that requires very little actual preparation. These are the creation
of Eli Dahlin, the original chef at The Walrus and the Carpenter, and appear
often on the menu there.

For information on buying boquerones, see Resources, page 293.

1 cup (2 sticks) unsalted butter,
  cold
2 dozen Baguette Toasts
  (page 278)

24 deboned, filleted oil-packed
  boquerones (from a 7-ounce
  package), drained
⅓ cup freshly grated horseradish,
  from a 4-inch piece
3 tablespoons *ikura* (salmon roe)

✦ Just before serving, use a cheese grater or vegetable peeler (or a sharp knife)
to shave the butter into ⅛-inch-thick slices. Cover each piece of toast with butter
shavings (they will look like cheese slices), then top each with 1 fish (2 joined
fillets), a big pinch (about ½ teaspoon) of the horseradish, and a tiny pile (a heaping ¼ teaspoon) of ikura. Serve immediately.

boat street chicken liver pâté
pickled shallots

PREP TIME: 30 MINUTES // TOTAL TIME: 24 HOURS // MAKES ABOUT 4 CUPS
SPECIAL EQUIPMENT: 8-BY-4-INCH LOAF PAN

AT THE WALRUS AND THE CARPENTER and at Barnacle, we serve different pâtés in little glass pots, often topped directly with pickles. But at Boat Street Café and The Whale Wins, we serve it the same way it's been served since Susan Kaplan, Boat Street's original owner, taught me to make it when I first worked there: in big slabs, smoothed until perfectly flat with the sharp edge of a knife.

This pâté is also delicious with Boat Street Pickles' French Plum pickles (see Resources, page 293) or a pot of smooth Dijon mustard.

NOTE: Because freshly grated nutmeg has a much brighter, cleaner flavor than its preground cousin, I highly recommend you buy nutmegs whole and grate them yourself.

---

1 cup (2 sticks) unsalted butter, softened, divided
1 medium onion, finely chopped
3 cloves garlic, finely chopped
1 pound organic chicken livers
3 tablespoons tawny port
1 teaspoon kosher salt
¼ cup loosely packed dried currants
¼ cup heavy cream
1 tablespoon dry mustard

½ teaspoon freshly grated nutmeg
⅛ teaspoon cayenne pepper
2 dozen Baguette Toasts (page 278) or Grilled Bread (page 277), for serving
Simplest Pickled Shallots (page 222), for serving
Flaky sea salt, such as Maldon or Jacobsen (see Resources, page 293), for finishing

✦ In a large sauté pan over medium heat, melt 1 stick of the butter. Add the onion and garlic and cook, stirring, for 3 minutes. Add the livers and port, season with the salt, and cook for 6 to 8 minutes, carefully turning the livers and rearranging them in the pan a few times so they all cook evenly on both sides. Remove the pan from the heat and let cool for 5 minutes.

✦ Transfer the liver and onion to a heavy-duty blender or food processor, along with the remaining 1 stick butter, currants, cream, dry mustard, nutmeg, and cayenne. Whirl on high speed until completely smooth, 3 to 5 minutes for a regular home blender, then pour the pâté into a fine-mesh strainer set over a mixing bowl. Use a rubber spatula to press the mixture through the strainer and into the bowl.

✦ Line an 8-by-4-inch loaf pan with plastic wrap. Pour the strained pâté into the pan, then gently knock the pan on the counter a few times to release any air bubbles. Carefully place another layer of plastic wrap directly onto the surface of the pâté. Chill the pâté until firm, preferably overnight.

✦ To serve, carefully invert the pâté onto a cutting board. Peel back the plastic wrap and use a large knife to cut two 2- to 3-inch slabs off the loaf. (Using a knife that's been run under warm water, then dried, will produce a prettier surface.)

✦ Transfer each slab to a platter. Serve the pâté cold, with toasted bread, pickled shallots, and a sprinkling of the sea salt.

✦ If you prefer to make the pâté in smaller portions, transfer the pâté to small jars, instead of the loaf pan, cover the surface of the pâté directly with plastic, and chill until firm. Serve right from the jars. The pâté will keep, refrigerated, for up to 10 days.

seared scallops

crème fraîche, herring roe, dill

PREP TIME: 30 MINUTES // TOTAL TIME: 30 MINUTES // SERVES 12

WHAT I LIKE ABOUT THIS RICH, indulgent appetizer is the combination of textures. In each bite of a giant scallop, you get that silky meat, seared crisp on the outside but still meltingly tender inside, and the pop of the roe. Herring roe is similar in texture to *tobiko*, but it has a lovely pale-yellow color. (If you ever get a chance, try it dried, on kelp. In Alaska, fishermen hang kelp near the shore in pens, and when the herring spawn, the eggs stick to the kelp. Dried, the roe makes the kelp actually sparkle.)

It's important to get fresh (never frozen) dry-packed scallops, if possible, from Alaska, British Columbia, or Maine. Dry-packed scallops aren't infused with water, so they brown better and have a more intense flavor. I also dry my scallops on a kitchen towel, rather than a paper towel, because real cloth tends to absorb more moisture. For more information on where to buy scallops, see Resources, page 293.

You can use two pans for the scallops, if you prefer. Just make sure you baste quickly, so that both batches of scallops benefit from an extra layer of caramelization from the hot butter.

NOTE: Use leftover herring roe to top the crêpes from the Gâteau de Crêpes (page 78), made without the sugar and rolled around crème fraîche and dill.

---

6 tablespoons (¾ stick) unsalted
   butter, divided
2 tablespoons extra-virgin olive oil,
   divided
12 U/10 dry-packed scallops
   (about 1½ pounds), tabs
   removed, patted dry with a towel
Kosher salt
1 medium lemon, halved

1½ cups crème fraîche
½ cup herring roe (from a
   10.5-ounce jar)
½ cup fresh dill, picked off the
   stems
Flaky sea salt, such as Maldon or
   Jacobsen (see Resources, page
   293), for finishing

✦ Heat a large stainless-steel pan over medium-high heat. When hot, add 2 tablespoons of the butter and 1 tablespoon of the oil to the pan.

✦ While the butter melts, season the scallops on both flat sides with kosher salt. When the butter is melted and bubbling, add 6 scallops to the pan, moving each scallop back and forth in the fat a few times before letting it go so that the fat gets into the cracks of each one. Brown the scallops, untouched, for 3 to 4 minutes on the first side, or until they are toasty brown and release easily from the pan. Using tongs, turn the scallops, and add another tablespoon of butter to the pan.

Using a serving spoon, baste the scallops with the butter constantly for 2 minutes, until the second side is browned. Squeeze half of the lemon over the scallops, then transfer the scallops to a paper towel–lined plate. Wipe the pan out with paper towels and repeat with the remaining butter, oil, scallops, and lemon.

✦ To serve the scallops, smear the crème fraîche on little individual plates, about 2 tablespoons per plate, or spread all of it onto one large platter. Place the scallops on the crème fraîche, then top each scallop with a heaping teaspoon of the roe and a big pinch of fresh dill. Garnish with a tiny bit of sea salt and serve immediately.

gâteau de crêpes

marmalade, whipped cream

**PREP TIME: 1½ HOURS // TOTAL TIME: 2½ HOURS // SERVES 12
SPECIAL EQUIPMENT: STEEL CRÊPE PAN**

YOU NEED TWO THINGS TO MAKE a crêpe cake, which consists of about 30 layers of classic French crêpes stacked with thin smears of good orange marmalade: time and patience. To simplify the process a bit—and to avoid rushing when I'm layering the crêpes with the marmalade—I often make the crêpes a week ahead and freeze them between layers of waxed paper, well wrapped in plastic wrap. I let them thaw in the refrigerator for at least a full day before assembling the cake.

You can make any size crêpes you wish. Obviously the larger the pan, the fewer crêpes, but note that smaller crêpes mean a taller, more impressive cake.

NOTE: Cooking crêpes is an art that a cook improves upon each time the pan is used; don't expect the first crêpe to be perfect. You may need to thin or thicken the batter or adjust the heat as necessary; the crêpes should be lightly browned and just thick enough to hold together when you transfer them to the plate. The beauty of this cake is that even the ugly crêpes can be used. About six crêpes into the process, I usually start watching a movie.

2¼ cups whole milk
2¼ cups water
2 cups (4 sticks) unsalted butter, melted, plus more for greasing the pan
9 large egg yolks
5 tablespoons granulated sugar, divided

1½ teaspoons kosher salt
3 cups (about 384 grams) all-purpose flour
3 cups orange marmalade
2 cups heavy cream, for whipping
Confectioners' sugar, for dusting

✦ First, make the crêpe batter: In a blender, whirl together the milk, water, 2 cups melted butter, egg yolks, 3 tablespoons of the granulated sugar, and salt until smooth. Add the flour and pulse until just incorporated. Transfer the batter to a bowl and let it rest for at least 1 hour, or refrigerate, covered, overnight. (If you don't have a monster-size blender, you may have to do this in two batches, stirring them together in the bowl before refrigerating.)

✦ To cook the crêpes, heat a 6-inch (or similar) steel crêpe pan over medium heat. When it's hot, brush the pan liberally with melted butter, then add a scant ¼ cup of batter, turning and twisting the pan until the batter has spread across the pan in an even layer. Let the crêpe cook for about 90 seconds, or until the center begins to bubble and the cooked side is marked with light-brown spots. Gently turn the crêpe (a flexible fish spatula or offset icing spatula works well) and cook another 30 to 60 seconds, until the second side is brown. Transfer the crêpe to a plate and repeat with the remaining batter, buttering the pan again between every few crêpes and sliding sheets of waxed paper between each crêpe so they don't stick together on the plate.

✦ To assemble the cake, place a sturdy-looking crêpe on a large, round platter or cake stand. Smear about 2 tablespoons of the marmalade evenly across the cake, then add another crêpe. Repeat with the remaining marmalade and crêpes, ending with a crêpe, and smear any remaining marmalade onto the sides of the cake. Transfer the platter to the refrigerator and chill for at least 1 hour, or up to 24 hours, before serving.

✦ To prepare the cream: In the work bowl of a stand mixer fitted with the whisk attachment, whip the cream on medium-high speed for 1 minute. Add the remaining 2 tablespoons sugar, then whip until the cream forms soft peaks, another minute or two.

✦ To serve, dust the cake with confectioners' sugar, cut into slices, and plate with puffs of the whipped cream.

SPRING

Wild Foods Dinner

Grilled Oysters *89*
Snail Butter

Roasted Side of Halibut *91*
Morel Cream, Sautéed Morels

Lentil Salad *94*
Nettles, Mustard Seed Oil, Currants, Tarragon

Watercress Salad *97*
Simple Honey Vinegar Dressing

Strawberry Jam Tart *98*

SERVES 8

SPRING, IN SEATTLE, is the temperamental love child of January and July. But as the days hopscotch between frigid and downright tropical, the ground begins its slow, dependable march toward the growing season. And nowhere is that walk more delicious than in the wilds of Washington.

At our restaurants, spring menus are packed with short-lived goodies from our region's foragers. From stinging nettles—the aptly named greens whose prickly tendencies subside when they are cooked—to morel mushrooms, we look forward to spring's fleeting ingredients with hearty anticipation.

ADAM JAMES AND LISSA JAMES MONBERG, HAMA HAMA COMPANY

The narrow bridges that span the two forks of the Hamma Hamma River, built in the '20s, look like the kinds of things that might survive for centuries, if the modern car's sideview mirror weren't such an issue. South of the two, near the town of Eldon on northwestern Washington's Hood Canal, is the Hama Hama Company.

Siblings Adam James and Lissa James Monberg manage the oyster farm with a two-pronged approach that combines tumbled and beach-grown bivalves. They hand-harvest lay-flat specimens (those that grow directly on the canal floor) at low tide, but since 2006, they've also turned to more modern oystering techniques. Now they can produce 3 to 4 million oysters each year with exactly the flavor profiles their customers want. Growing tumbled oysters, for example—which are farmed about two feet above the seabed in mesh bags that get drained at low tide—has enabled the company to produce exceptionally clean-tasting oysters that are reliably gorgeous.

Four generations (and the addition of an oyster farm) since its 1922 founding as a timber company, the Hama Hama Company now produces Pacific and Olympia oysters (and butter, savory, and Manila clams as well) on 180 acres of tideland. It's most well-known for natural-set, seed-grown heritage Hama Hamas, which have a bright, cucumber-tinted finish; tumbled Blue Pools, with their exceptional vegetal, almost carroty flavor; and Block Bs, which are grown using a hybrid of the two methods. The family still owns the timberland bordering the lower stretches of the river; beyond their trees, the land is publicly owned, which means they can operate knowing their oysters have very limited contact with pesticides—an unusual advantage, proven by their oysters' remarkable flavor.

There are vague plans to replace those narrow Hamma Hamma bridges with modern ones. Appropriate symbols for the company, the bridges link traditional and modern farming techniques, old generations and new. In the meantime, The Walrus and the Carpenter takes all the Blue Pool oysters Adam and Lissa will sell us.

grilled oysters

snail butter

PREP TIME: 35 MINUTES, PLUS SHUCKING TIME // TOTAL TIME: 45 MINUTES // SERVES 8

MORE THAN THE FLAVOR OF HAMA HAMA Oyster Company's oysters, or the fact that it's a long-standing family business, or that it's a perfect example of why Puget Sound shellfish make me proud of my region, I love the company because it's passionate about its product. Twinkly-eyed sales manager Danial Crookston wooed me with its classic Hama Hamas; I love a good fluted natural oyster because it has a softer, more varied texture than a tumbled oyster and often a more complex flavor. (I also happen to love the oyster salesman for similar reasons.)

Because the farm is wedged between the towering Olympic Mountains and the deep, icy waters of Hood Canal, the sun sets early at Hama Hama. It's a good thing; it's one of the canal's most productive oystering spots, and much of the work is done early each morning. For farmers like Nick James, who's often the first one to head out on the oyster barge, an early sunset means early dinner— sometimes consisting entirely of oysters like these, which are shucked and grilled on the half shell with garlicky green snail butter.

Don't panic; there are no snails in this butter. I call it that simply because it's a version of what's traditionally loaded onto French escargots. Both Hama Hama oysters and escargots have very vegetal qualities, so the flavors transfer beautifully.

Stir any leftover snail butter into scrambled eggs, or serve it atop grilled steak.

2 cups (4 sticks) unsalted butter, softened
3 cloves garlic, roughly chopped
1 tablespoon Dijon mustard
½ cup capers (salt-packed preferred), rinsed well (see Capers, page 188)
Grated zest of 1 large lemon

⅓ cup freshly squeezed lemon juice (from about 2 large lemons)
2 cups loosely packed fresh Italian parsley leaves
1 cup loosely packed mint leaves
Kosher salt and freshly ground black pepper
2 dozen oysters, each about 2½ to 3½ inches long

✦ Melt the butter in a saucepan over low heat. When about half the butter has melted, transfer it to the work bowl of a food processor or heavy-duty blender. Add the garlic, mustard, capers, lemon zest and juice, parsley, mint, and salt and pepper to taste. Whirl on high speed until smooth and bright green. Transfer the butter to a bowl and set aside.

✦ Prepare a charcoal or gas grill for cooking over medium-high heat, about 425 degrees F. Brush the cooking grates clean.

continued

→ Shuck the oysters, leaving the oyster meat and liquor in the deep half of the shell per the oyster-shucking instructions on page 232. (If the shell is more than half full of liquid, tip some of the liquid out; you want the oysters to roast, not boil.) Top each raw oyster with about 1½ teaspoons of the butter. Place them on the grill and cook until the butter melts and begins to brown at the edges and the oyster's muscle contracts, 8 to 10 minutes for medium-size oysters. Serve immediately.

roasted side of halibut

morel cream, sautéed morels

PREP TIME: 45 MINUTES // TOTAL TIME: 1 HOUR 30 MINUTES // SERVES 8

IN MY OPINION, THERE ARE TWO common misconceptions about fish: first, that it needs to be served hot, and second, that it should be parsed out in neat, skinny pieces. When fresh halibut hits our markets each spring, I roast it in a big slab and serve it in the jagged hunks it breaks into naturally, with a rich morel-studded cream that tastes just as lovely at room temperature as it does right out of the oven. Be sure to save the lemony tonic left in the baking tray after you transfer the fish to a serving platter; it makes the most perfect dipping sauce for the requisite last-minute bread dipping a responsible dishwasher turns to partway through cleanup.

If you're going to spend a lot of money on a side of halibut—which you'll need to do for this feast—make sure you get what you want. Ask for a center cut of the fish that's roughly the same thickness from one end to the other. Three and a half pounds will serve eight people comfortably; buy less for light eaters.

Note that the morel cream that garnishes the fish needs to be started about an hour before you cook the fish; it can also be made ahead and reheated when the halibut comes out of the oven, but it's best to sauté the morels just before serving.

¾ pound fresh (not dried) morel mushrooms

2 cups heavy cream

1 medium leek, white and light-green parts, washed well and roughly chopped

2 fresh bay leaves

Stripped peel of 1 lemon

½ teaspoon kosher salt, plus more for seasoning

1 (3- to 3½-pound) side fresh halibut

Freshly ground black pepper

2 whole lemons, quartered

4 tablespoons unsalted butter, divided

Fresh herb sprigs, such as watercress or chervil, for garnish

Flaky sea salt, such as Maldon or Jacobsen (see Resources, page 293), for finishing

✦ First, clean the mushrooms: Using a small, sharp knife, cut the stems off the mushrooms about ¼ inch into each mushroom cap, separating the caps and stems into two separate bowls and halving any mushrooms that are bigger than a

continued

thumb. Wash the mushrooms and ends thoroughly in many changes of water (as many as five for really dirty specimens) and drain well on cloth towels.

✦ Place the mushroom stems and about a quarter of the mushroom caps (I usually choose the biggest pieces) in a large saucepan along with the cream, leeks, bay leaves, lemon peel, and ½ teaspoon salt. Bring the mixture to a strong simmer over high heat, then reduce the heat and cook at a bare simmer for about 45 minutes, stirring occasionally, until the vegetables are soft and the cream has reduced a bit. Discard the bay leaves. In the work bowl of a blender or food processor, whirl the morel cream until very smooth. (You can strain the cream here, if desired.) Season to taste with additional salt, if necessary, and set aside.

✦ Preheat the oven to 400 degrees F. Place the fish in a large baking pan or on a rimmed baking sheet. When the morel cream is done, smear the fillet evenly with ½ cup of it, season to taste with salt and pepper, and scatter the lemons around the fish in the pan.

✦ Roast the fish for 25 to 30 minutes, or until just cooked through in the center. About 10 minutes before the fish is done, heat a large sauté pan over medium-high heat. Add 2 tablespoons of the butter. When the butter has melted, add half the remaining morels and season to taste with salt. Cook, stirring occasionally, until the mushrooms are soft and have given up their water, 5 to 10 minutes. Transfer the mushrooms and water to a bowl and repeat with the remaining butter and mushrooms. Pour any water off the mushrooms. Stir a big handful of the sautéed mushrooms into the morel cream, and rewarm the cream, if necessary.

✦ Squeeze the lemons over the cooked fish and discard. Slide the spatula between the fish and the skin to release the flesh, then, using the spatula or your hands, gently break the fish apart into serving pieces by bending it until it breaks naturally.

✦ Transfer the fish pieces to a serving plate. Drape the fish with the remaining morel cream and top with the sautéed morels. Garnish with the herbs, sprinkle with the sea salt, and serve, hot or at room temperature.

lentil salad

nettles, mustard seed oil, currants, tarragon

PREP TIME: 30 MINUTES ACTIVE TIME // TOTAL TIME: 1 HOUR 30 MINUTES
SERVES 8 TO 10

WHEN YOU COOK LENTILS, THERE'S AN earthy perfume that pervades the kitchen. That smell has been an addiction of mine for as long as I can remember; in my home, lentils are a staple.

Nettles blanket the forest floors (and many backyards) near Seattle each spring. To use them, put on a pair of gardening gloves and carefully pick the leaves off. Their stinging properties disappear when they hit the heat of the pan, but before then, be cautious; they're called stinging nettles for a reason. If you can't find nettles, use kale or mustard greens (with the ribs removed, and roughly chopped).

2 cups Beluga lentils, rinsed and picked over

6 cups chicken or vegetable stock

¾ cup dried black currants

½ cup sherry or cognac

2 tablespoons unsalted butter

3 large shallots, cut into ⅛-inch rings (1 heaping cup sliced)

8 cups firmly packed nettle leaves

1 cup extra-virgin olive oil, plus more for seasoning

⅓ cup champagne vinegar (see Resources, page 293), plus more for seasoning

1 tablespoon kosher salt, plus more for seasoning

Julienned peel of 2 large lemons

1 cup loosely packed whole tarragon leaves (no stems)

2 cups whole walnuts, toasted (see Toasting Nuts, page 12)

2 tablespoons mustard seed oil (see Resources, page 293), plus more to taste

✦ Combine the lentils and stock in a large pot and bring to a boil over high heat. Reduce the heat and simmer until just tender, 10 to 15 minutes. (Note: These lentils cook very fast. You want them cooked through but not mushy.) Drain the lentils and spread them out on a sheet pan to cool for about 30 minutes.

✦ Meanwhile, combine the currants and sherry or cognac in a small bowl and set aside.

✦ Heat a large sauté pan over medium heat. When hot, add the butter, then the shallots, and cook, stirring occasionally, until they are transparent, about 2 minutes. Add the nettles and about a cup of water. (Use just ½ cup water if using other greens.) Cover until the water boils, then cook, stirring the nettles with tongs so they cook evenly, until the nettles are soft and dark green, 3 to 5 minutes.

(If you're using other greens, cook until the water is almost gone.) Set the shallots and nettles aside to cool for about 20 minutes, then drain off any excess liquid.

✦ In a large bowl, combined the cooled lentils, shallots, nettles, and olive oil. Drain the booze off the currants and add the currants to the mixture, along with the vinegar and 1 tablespoon salt. Stir the ingredients together and check for seasoning—lentils tend to need a lot of dressing, so don't be shy with the salt, oil, and vinegar. Stir in the lemon zest.

✦ Just before serving, fold in the tarragon and walnuts, and drizzle with the mustard seed oil, adding more to taste. Serve at room temperature.

watercress salad

simple honey vinegar dressing

PREP TIME: 10 MINUTES // TOTAL TIME: 10 MINUTES // SERVES 8

WHEN SPRING HAS SPRUNG, AND STRONG, spindly greens first pepper the farmers' markets, I begin to crave watercress. Picked wild—inevitably from brambly banks of a pool of water that reminds me I'm wearing the wrong shoes for picking—it has an even sharper flavor, which is why I dress it simply, with a soft honey vinegar, good extra-virgin olive oil, and sea salt.

If you can't find wild watercress (ask your local forager), wild baby arugula is a better substitute than hydroponic watercress, because it has a similarly strong, peppery flavor.

I buy Italian honey vinegar (see Resources, page 293). If you can't find it, you can also mix champagne vinegar with 1 tablespoon good honey.

6 ounces wild watercress, tough
   stems removed
¼ cup soft extra-virgin olive oil
2 tablespoons honey vinegar

Flaky sea salt, such as Maldon or
   Jacobsen (see Resources, page
   293), for finishing

✦ Put the clean watercress in a large, wide bowl. Just before serving, drizzle with the oil and vinegar, and garnish with salt.

SPRING FLOWERS

I find spring almost unbearably exciting. I like how violent the season can be here in Seattle; every piece of life gets reborn, from the tiniest ground crocuses to the tips of the biggest cherry trees, and the air is filled with hope. Historically, we've always put spring branches in the restaurants as decoration because they're timeless and beautiful and encouraging. I start with a large metal can or pickle crock filled with rocks. I add just one type of tree branch at a time—my favorites are apple, plum, cherry, lilac, and magnolia—but I don't ever mix tree types, because each has its own stunning beauty. I shove the branches into the rocks to keep them upright, then add water and let them bloom. (It's also nice that if you smash the bottoms before you put them in water, they force beautiful leaves and flowers that last a good long while.)

strawberry jam tart

PREP TIME: 30 MINUTES // TOTAL TIME: ABOUT 2 HOURS // SERVES 8
SPECIAL EQUIPMENT: 9-INCH FLUTED TART PAN WITH A REMOVABLE BOTTOM,
OR A 9-INCH SPRINGFORM PAN

AT THE OLD BOAT STREET CAFÉ, my mom made all the desserts—brownies, pound cakes, tart shells, everything. One day, I unlocked the front door around 7 a.m., heading to the back door, where flats of strawberries and my mother's tart shells sat waiting for me to use for the day's sweets. Out of the corner of my eye, I caught a man dashing toward the back door, heading to steal our desserts. I flew through the dining room and the kitchen, and slammed my body into the back door. It scared him away with only a few tart shells and a slice of my dignity. Every time I make this tart—it's best with jam made from the season's first sweet strawberries—I take a moment to be thankful when the tart actually makes it onto the table.

½ cup (1 stick) plus 2 tablespoons unsalted butter, softened
½ cup granulated sugar
2 large eggs, divided
1 large egg yolk
⅛ teaspoon almond extract
1½ cups (about 192 grams) all-purpose flour, plus more for rolling out the dough

½ cup medium stone-ground cornmeal or polenta
2 teaspoons baking powder
1 teaspoon kosher salt
1 (16-ounce) jar strawberry jam (about 1¾ cups)
2 tablespoons demerara sugar (see Resources, page 293)
Heavy cream, for serving

✦ In a stand mixer fitted with the paddle attachment, cream the butter and sugar together on medium speed until light, about 1 minute. Add 1 of the eggs, the egg yolk, and the almond extract, and blend again on medium speed until combined, scraping down the sides as needed with a rubber spatula.

✦ In a separate bowl, whisk together the flour, cornmeal, baking powder, and salt. With the mixer on low speed, add the dry ingredients in 2 or 3 separate additions, mixing just until no dry spots remain.

✦ Divide the dough into two equal sections, press the hunks of dough into 6-inch disks, wrap in plastic wrap or waxed paper, and chill both disks for about 1 hour.

✦ Preheat the oven to 350 degrees F.

✦ On a floured surface, roll one piece of dough into a roughly 10-inch circle about ¼ inch thick. (If your dough has chilled more than an hour, let it rest for a few minutes on the counter before rolling.) Transfer the dough to the pan, then press the dough into the sides of the tart pan with your fingers, pushing it all the way up to the top edge if you're using a fluted pan, or about 1 inch up the edge if you're using a springform pan. Spread the jam into the tart shell in a roughly even layer. Roll the remaining piece of dough to ¼ inch thick, and use a shot glass (or similar 1¼-inch circle cutter) to stamp out as many circle shapes as possible, rerolling the dough as necessary. Arrange the circles on the jam in any pattern that seems pleasing to you. I tend to arrange them in two circles, one around the outside of the tart and one around the inside, with the edges overlapping slightly, but anything works. (Note that on a warm day, it may be easier to roll out the dough between two lightly floured sheets of waxed paper.)

✦ Whisk together the remaining egg and 1 tablespoon water, brush it onto the top crust, and sprinkle the crust with the demerara sugar.

✦ Bake the tart on the middle rack of the oven until the pastry is golden brown, about 30 minutes. Serve the tart warm, with heavy cream poured over it.

🌿 Spring Ingredients 🌿

ASPARAGUS

Asparagus with Julia's Blender Hollandaise and Chervil

✦ In a blender, whirl together **3 large egg yolks, 2 tablespoons freshly squeezed lemon juice**, and **½ teaspoon kosher salt** until well blended and one shade lighter in color. While the blender is going, drizzle in **1 cup (2 sticks) melted butter**, adding water as necessary if the sauce gets too thick. Season to taste with additional salt and lemon juice, then pulse in **¼ cup finely chopped fresh chervil**. Drape the sauce over **2 pounds grilled or steamed trimmed asparagus**. *Serves 8.*

Chilled Asparagus Soup with Yogurt

✦ In a large skillet, sauté **2 pounds chopped, trimmed asparagus** in **2 tablespoons extra-virgin olive oil** until bright, about 3 minutes. Add water until it comes halfway up the sides of the asparagus—about 1 cup, but note that you want them to steam, rather than boil—and cook, covered, until tender, about 5 minutes more. Blend until smooth with **2 tablespoons chopped fresh mint** (you may need to add a bit of water to get the asparagus to move), then pulse in **2 cups whole milk yogurt**, season to taste with **kosher salt**, and chill. Taste again for seasoning when the soup is cold, then serve with a **drizzle of olive oil**. *Serves 2 to 4.*

Roasted Asparagus with Mashed Avocado, Poached Egg, and Mustard Seed Oil

✦ In a roasting pan, toss **1 pound trimmed asparagus** with **1 tablespoon olive oil** and **kosher salt to taste**. Roast at 450 degrees F for 6 to 8 minutes, until bright, and set aside. Mash the flesh of **1 ripe avocado** until chunky and smear it onto a serving plate. Top with the asparagus, then drizzle with **1 to 2 teaspoons mustard seed oil** (see Resources, page 293) and the **juice of 1 small lime**. Season with **flaky sea salt** and top with **1 poached egg**. *Serves 2 to 4.*

FAVA BEANS

Fava Bean, Pea, and Spring Onion Potato Salad with Mint

✦ Smear **Green Goddess Dressing** (page 191) on the bottom of a serving plate. In a mixing bowl, toss together **1 cup cooked fava beans** (from 1 pound beans with their shells), **1 cup cooked fresh peas**, **2 small grilled onions**, and **1 pound steamed baby potatoes** with a drizzle of **extra-virgin olive oil**. Scoop the vegetables onto the dressing, then garnish with **flaky sea salt** and **¼ cup torn fresh mint leaves**. *Serves 4 to 6.*

Grilled Whole Favas over Ricotta with Honey, Lime, and Aleppo Pepper

✦ String **1 pound whole fava beans** without removing the shell. Toss with **¼ cup extra-virgin olive oil** and grill over high heat until blistered and soft, turning once or twice, about 5 minutes total. Toss again with **2 tablespoons olive oil**, **flaky sea salt**, **2 tablespoons honey**, **juice of 1 lime**, and **Aleppo pepper** to taste. Serve on a puddle of **Ricotta** (page 287). *Serves 4 to 6.*

Puréed Favas with Olive Oil and Garlic

✦ Shuck **2½ pounds fava beans**. Blanch the beans 2 minutes in boiling water, shock in ice water, peel, and cook in simmering water until soft, about another 2 minutes. (You'll have a scant 2 cups cooked beans.) In a blender or food processor, puree the beans with **¾ cup extra-virgin olive oil**, **1 finely chopped garlic clove**, and **flaky sea salt** to taste. Spread the puree on **Baguette Toasts** (page 278) and top with **shaved radishes** and **flaky sea salt**, or smear on a plate and use as a base for grilled fish. *Makes about 2 cups.*

NETTLES

Nettle Pesto with Walnuts

✦ Blanch **4 cups nettles** for 2 minutes in boiling salted water, drain, submerge in ice water, drain again, then squeeze the water out. In a food processor, whirl the nettles with **½ cup toasted walnuts**, **2 cloves thinly sliced garlic**, **juice of 1 large lemon**, and **Pecorino Romano cheese** to taste (about ½ cup) until smooth. With the machine running, add about **¾ cup olive oil**, then season to taste with **sea salt**. Serve with a side of poached salmon. *Serves 8.*

Nettle Tart with Pine Nuts and Ricotta

✦ In a large skillet, cook **1 sliced large onion** in **1 tablespoon olive oil** over medium heat until deep golden brown, about 45 minutes, stirring frequently. Blanch **3 cups nettles** for 2 minutes in boiling salted water, drain, and squeeze the water out. In a mixing bowl, whisk together **3 large eggs, 1 cup heavy cream, ½ cup grated Parmesan cheese, ½ teaspoon kosher salt**, and a generous grating of **fresh nutmeg**. Spread the onions into a tart pan lined with **Shirlee's Crust** (page 290). Place the nettles in tablespoon-size blobs on top of the onions, then fill the rest of the tart with **¾ cup ricotta cheese** scooped on in similar-size blobs. Pour in enough of the egg mixture to fill the tart, then scatter **¼ cup raw pine nuts** over the top. Place the pan on a baking sheet and bake at 350 degrees F for about 50 minutes, or until set in the center and golden brown on the edges. *Serves 6 to 8.*

Slow-Braised Nettle Soup with Ginger, Garlic, Leeks, Shallots, and Onions

✦ In a large soup pot, melt **2 tablespoons butter** over medium heat. Add **1 sliced onion, 2 sliced shallots, 1 sliced leek**, and **2 thinly sliced garlic cloves**. Cook over medium heat, stirring frequently, until soft, about 10 minutes. Add **1 pound nettles** and **4 cups water**, bring to a simmer, and cook over low heat for 30 minutes, stirring occasionally, or until the nettles are completely soft. (You may have to add the greens a little at a time at first, until the first greens soften.) Stir in a **½ loosely packed cup chopped fresh Italian parsley** (with the stems), **1 cup heavy cream**, and **2 tablespoons grated fresh ginger**, and blend until smooth. *Serves 8.*

RHUBARB

Pickled Rhubarb

✦ Cut **½ pound skinny rhubarb stalks** into 1-inch pieces and pack them into a pint-size canning jar. In a saucepan, combine **1 cup white wine vinegar, ¼ cup water, ¼ cup sugar, 1 fresh bay leaf, 2 peppercorns**, and **½ teaspoon kosher salt**. Bring the mixture to a simmer and cook for 2 to 3 minutes, stirring occasionally, until the sugar has dissolved. Pour the liquid over the rhubarb, let sit for 1 hour, then cover and refrigerate. Serve with charcuterie, or use in the **Lentil Salad** (page 94), finely chopped, in place of the raisins. *Makes about 2 cups.*

Raw Baby Rhubarb Topping

✦ I owe this one to the kitchen crew at Boat Street Café: Slice ½ **pound baby rhubarb** as thinly as possible at a 45-degree angle and toss with ¼ **cup sugar.** Let the mixture sit for about 30 minutes, then serve over vanilla ice cream. (Be sure you only use the season's first tender stalks.) *Serves 4.*

Rhubarb Tart

✦ Make the **Strawberry Jam Tart** (page 98), filling the center with rhubarb jam instead of strawberry jam. *Makes 1.*

SORREL

Cream of Sorrel and Potato Soup

✦ Clean and thinly slice **1 medium leek.** In a large pot over medium heat, melt **2 tablespoons unsalted butter,** then add the leeks and cook until very soft but not browned, stirring frequently, about 15 minutes. Add **3 fist-size peeled and quartered white potatoes (about 1½ pounds)** and ½ **pound sorrel,** then add **chicken stock** to cover (about 4 cups). Simmer the soup over low heat until the potatoes are totally soft, about 25 minutes. Stir in ½ **cup heavy cream** and ¼ **cup chopped Italian parsley,** with the stems, and cook another few minutes. Blend the soup, then season with **sea salt.** *Serves 4 to 6.*

Salmon with Sorrel Cream Sauce

✦ In a blender, whirl together ½ cup **sour cream,** ½ cup **heavy cream, 2 packed cups raw sorrel,** and **2 tablespoons olive oil** until evenly green. Season with **cayenne pepper** and **kosher salt** to taste (you can add a little water if it seems too thick), and serve over poached, grilled, or roasted **salmon,** with potatoes on the side. *Serves 6 to 8.*

Scrambled Eggs with Thinly Sliced Sorrel, Cracked Pepper, and Goat Cheese

✦ Scramble **8 large eggs** your favorite way, folding in **1 packed cup thinly sliced sorrel** and ½ **cup crumbled goat cheese** just before they set. Top with **cracked black pepper** before serving. *Serves 4.*

Lummi Island
Spot Prawn Dinner

Raw Spot Prawns *109*
Lime Zest, Olive Oil, Sea Salt

Messy Spot Prawns *111*
Slivered Garlic, Piment d'Espelette, Lemon, Butter

Steamed Artichokes *115*
Thyme Mayonnaise

Raw Asparagus Salad *116*
Mint and Parsley Pesto

Honeyed Rice Pudding Pots *117*
Wild Strawberries

SERVES 6 TO 8

I GREW UP SPENDING SUMMERS in a shack at Spee-Bi-Dah, near the Tulalip Indian Reservation, about an hour north of Seattle. Our little spot near the beach had no hot water, and the bathroom was outdoors, but we were free to roam as we pleased. Often, we walked to the point near Port Susan and watched tribal fishermen net king salmon, using their traditional low-impact, shore-based fishing method. As kids, when the sea life thrashed in the net as the fishermen hauled it in by hand, we thought the water was boiling. If we were lucky, they would let us help with the net and reward us with the smaller fish they couldn't sell. My brother, Ryan, and I would walk home with three or four fish strung on a stick between us.

Today, the fishing traditions in the Puget Sound are still strong. We frequently buy sockeye salmon for the restaurants from the Lummi Nation and halibut from the Lopez Tribe, in part because we try to buy the freshest fish we can find, and in part because I have a permanent nostalgia for their fishing customs.

Those summers also instilled in me an unrelenting eagerness to catch things myself. In Washington, geographical fishing regions open and close for different fish and shellfish catches as the Department of Fish and Wildlife deems necessary; they've developed a reputation as an excellent manager of Puget Sound waters. Spot prawns, which have a relatively short season each spring, are available to recreational shrimpers throughout the Puget Sound (and beyond), but I often fish for them off Lummi Island simply because it's a beautiful representation of our gorgeous region.

The catch is celebrated twice: once on the boat, with a cold beer and spot prawns eaten at their simplest—raw with lime zest, salt, and olive oil—then again as the sun sets, as part of a feast with friends. And the morning after, when the smell of spice has cleared the kitchen, we start the boat's engine again.

raw spot prawns
lime zest, olive oil, sea salt

PREP TIME: 15 MINUTES // TOTAL TIME: 15 MINUTES // SERVES 6 TO 8

IF YOU'RE GOING TO GO SPOT-PRAWNING during Washington's spring recreational shrimping season to find the rich, beautiful meat of a creature quite unique to the Pacific Northwest, you'll need a few things. You'll need a friend with a boat, for sure, and a fishing license, and traps and bait. But most importantly, you'll need a lime, a zesting tool, great olive oil, and flaky sea salt. On the waters off the north side of Orcas Island, nothing beats eating the first prawns raw, still ice-cold from the ocean, with three simple ingredients.

Your trip will also require cold Rainier beer, but whether you drink it before the traps come up, or only after the prawns are in the cooler, as some insist, is up to you.

NOTE: If you're buying frozen spot prawns, which often come in frozen blocks of seawater, defrost them in the fridge and eat them just as the chill is coming off.

---

24 fresh spot prawns, peeled
2 large limes
Soft extra-virgin olive oil, such as
  a Ligurian oil (see below), for
  drizzling

Flaky sea salt, such as Maldon or
  Jacobsen (see Resources, page
  293), for finishing

✦ Place the prawns on a large plate. Zest the limes directly onto the prawns, so the zest falls onto them in a fine, green snow. Squeeze the lime juice over the prawns, then drizzle them with the olive oil and sprinkle with salt. Serve immediately.

A NEW OIL TO TASTE

Most Ligurian olive oil is made with Taggiasca olives, whose oil is buttery and rich. It's the perfect complement to the natural butteriness of spot prawns. If you can't find one, substitute a lovely French olive oil.

Much like with late-fall wine releases in France, Italian olive oils have a big fall release period, where "new" olive oils—called *nuovo* or *novello* oils, depending on their region of origin—come to the market. These oils are meant to be consumed immediately. They're incredibly intense, usually grassy and peppery, but when combined with something creamy and smooth, like ice cream or a single raw scallop, they're sublime.

We often do a special olive oil dinner at Boat Street Café, where diners can taste through the new oils. You can do an olive oil tasting at home; pour small amounts of oil into tiny ramekins and serve with grilled bread.

messy spot prawns

slivered garlic, piment d'espelette, lemon, butter

PREP TIME: 15 MINUTES // TOTAL TIME: 20 MINUTES // SERVES 6 TO 8

WHEN I WAS A KID, a guy in a fishing boat would pull into the shore at Spee-Bi-Dah, WA, and blow a horn to announce his arrival. He'd set up his little onboard steamer and cook shrimp for the locals, which he sold in brown paper lunch bags. We'd sit on the shore and eat them, launching the tails back into the water as the waves lapped the sides of his beached boat.

That doesn't happen anymore, sadly, but it taught me that the best way to eat shrimp—or spot prawns, the shrimp available each spring up and down the West Coast—is with your hands. I season them with *piment d'Espelette*, which I discovered for the first time in a little *epicérie* in Paris about fifteen years ago.

Espelette is my desert island spice; floral, citrusy, and mildly spicy, it's made with a Basque chili that really has no substitute. See the Resources section (page 293) for more information on where to buy it.

Eat these prawns from the outside in, peeling and dredging them in the Espelette butter only once you've sucked every bit of seasoning from the shell. Serve with a crusty baguette and a wet towel for each guest, for finger wiping.

3 pounds spot prawns, shells left on
1 cup (2 sticks) unsalted butter, divided
Kosher salt, for finishing
4 large cloves garlic, peeled and very thinly sliced, divided

1 tablespoon plus 1 teaspoon piment d'Espelette (see Resources, page 293), divided
¼ cup freshly squeezed lemon juice (from about 2 medium lemons), divided
½ cup chives, snipped into ½-inch pieces

✦ Heat two large, heavy skillets over high heat. When hot, add 4 tablespoons of the butter to each pan. When the butter is melted and bubbling, add enough prawns to cover each pan in a single layer, using about half of them. (You don't want the prawns overcrowded because they need to brown, not steam.) Season them generously with salt and let them cook for 1 minute on the first side. Sprinkle the contents of each pan evenly with 1 clove's worth of garlic and 1 teaspoon of the piment d'Espelette, and flip them over in the pan. Add half a lemon's worth of juice to each pan (this will prevent the butter from browning too much), then cook for another minute or two, until the prawns curl and the shells begin to brown.

continued

+ Transfer the prawns and Espelette butter to a large platter, and repeat with the remaining butter, prawns, salt, garlic, piment d'Espelette, and lemon juice, letting the pan come back up to temperature between batches, if necessary.

+ Serve the prawns piping hot, garnished with the chives, and instruct people to peel and dip the prawns into the Espelette butter (see below).

EATING SPOT PRAWNS, SHRIMP, AND THEIR SHELLS

In my mind, the best part of a shrimp is its shell. That's where the flavor is, and spot prawns are no exception. When I started serving spot prawns at Boat Street Café, right when we opened the second location, I trained my staff to teach guests how to eat them. You should do the same for yours.

When you pick up a prawn, remember that half the flavor comes before you peel it. Start by making a mental commitment to getting a little messy. Suck on the open end of the shell first, then on the tail. Finally, uncurl the thing, so its legs are splayed out, the same way you used to eat an orange wedge when you were a kid. Only after you've sucked the juices and seasonings out of the legs can you peel and eat it.

I've been known to eat spots whole, spiky nose to tail, but it can be a dangerous experience if you don't chew well.

steamed artichokes

thyme mayonnaise

PREP TIME: 15 MINUTES // TOTAL TIME: 40 MINUTES // SERVES 6 TO 8

WE ATE STEAMED ARTICHOKES ALL THE time growing up, usually on the beach with mayonnaise seasoned with just lemon. I make a mean homemade aioli, but for this dish, which always reminds me of eating artichokes with my parents, I prefer using good jarred mayonnaise, mostly for nostalgic purposes.

For a minted mayonnaise, substitute 1 cup loosely packed mint leaves for the parsley and omit the thyme.

NOTE: Be sure to make the thyme mayonnaise a few hours ahead of time, so the flavors have a chance to mingle together in the refrigerator.

---

1 (15-ounce) jar mayonnaise, such as Best Foods

1 loosely packed cup fresh Italian parsley, with stems

¼ cup loosely packed chopped thyme

Zest and juice of 1 large lemon

1 tablespoon extra-virgin olive oil (one with a grassy flavor is best), plus more for drizzling

½ teaspoon kosher salt

3 (1-pound) artichokes

+ In the work bowl of a food processor or heavy-duty blender, puree the mayonnaise, parsley, thyme, lemon zest, lemon juice, olive oil, and salt until pale green and smooth. Transfer to a bowl, cover, and refrigerate for a few hours, or up to 1 day, or until you're ready to serve the artichokes.

+ To steam the artichokes, trim the stem of each flat end to 1 inch below the base of each artichoke. Snuggle the artichokes into a large, heavy pot just big enough to hold them and fill the bottom of the pot with about 1½ inches of water. Bring the water to a simmer and cook, covered, for 25 to 30 minutes, until a leaf comes out without much resistance. (The meat at the end of each leaf should be tender.)

+ Serve the artichokes hot, at room temperature, or chilled, with the mayonnaise alongside, drizzled with a bit more olive oil.

raw asparagus salad

mint and parsley pesto

PREP TIME: 20 MINUTES // TOTAL TIME: 20 MINUTES // SERVES 6 TO 8

ASPARAGUS IS THE ULTIMATE SIGN OF spring. To a cook, it's a harbinger of good things to come after months of kale and potatoes. This salad brings out the sweetness and grassy flavor of the season's first asparagus. Make it only with the freshest local stalks you can find, and only in the spring.

Since you'll need toasted pine nuts for both the salad and the pesto, toast them together in a 350-degree oven for 5 to 10 minutes, or until lightly browned and fragrant.

for the SALAD:
2 cups golden raisins
2 pounds fresh asparagus, ends trimmed
1½ cups pine nuts, toasted
4 radishes, trimmed, halved, and thinly sliced

for the PESTO:
2 cups loosely packed fresh mint leaves
1½ cups extra-virgin olive oil

1½ cups loosely packed grated Parmesan cheese
1 cup loosely packed fresh Italian parsley, with stems
½ cup pine nuts, toasted
2 small garlic cloves, thinly sliced
2 tablespoons freshly squeezed lemon juice (from about 1 medium lemon)
1½ teaspoons kosher salt

✦ Start the salad: Place the raisins in a bowl and add boiling water to cover. Set the raisins aside to plump and soften.

✦ While the raisins soak, make the pesto: In a food processor or heavy-duty blender, whirl the mint, olive oil, Parmesan, parsley, pine nuts, garlic, lemon juice, and salt together until very smooth.

✦ Slice the asparagus very thinly on the bias, so each piece is about 2 inches long, and transfer them to a large bowl. Drain and add the raisins, then add the pine nuts and about 2 cups of the pesto, and stir to combine. (It should be liberally dressed but not soupy.) Serve the salad on a large platter, garnished with the sliced radishes.

honeyed rice pudding pots

wild strawberries

PREP TIME: 10 MINUTES ACTIVE, PLUS STIRRING // TOTAL TIME: 1 HOUR

SERVES 6 TO 8

INSPIRED BY THE RICE PUDDING AT L'Ami Jean, a restaurant in Paris, this ultra-creamy version can be eaten warm or cold. I personally prefer it cool, which means that it's the perfect make-ahead dessert to take with you on an adventure. In the summer, serve it with the tiny fresh wild strawberries that pop out at farmers' markets toward the end of spring. If you can't find them, substitute a good strawberry jam.

NOTE: If you'd prefer a strong vanilla flavor, stir the seeds of a whole split vanilla bean into the rice with the salt in lieu of the vanilla extract.

---

1 cup arborio rice

2¼ cups whole milk, plus ⅓ cup additional milk if serving cold

3 cups heavy cream, plus ⅓ cup additional cream if serving cold

1½ teaspoons vanilla extract

¼ teaspoon kosher salt

¼ cup plus 2 tablespoons local honey

2 tablespoons sugar

1 pint tiny wild strawberries, if available, halved if large

+ Bring a large pot of water to a boil. Add the rice, cook for 10 seconds to rid it of its external layer of starch, drain, and return the rice to the pot. Add the 2¼ cups milk, 3 cups cream, vanilla, and salt, and stir to combine. Cook the rice mixture over medium heat, or at a bare simmer, for 30 to 40 minutes, stirring occasionally, until the rice is just cooked and most of the liquid has been absorbed. Stir in the honey and sugar.

+ If you prefer the pudding warm, let it sit for 15 to 20 minutes to firm up, then serve it immediately in small jars or short cups.

+ If you prefer it cold, stir in the remaining ⅓ cup each of milk and cream, let it cool to room temperature, then refrigerate until it is cool and has the consistency of cottage cheese. Transfer the pudding to jars once it has cooled completely.

+ Serve the puddings topped with the strawberries.

CORKY LUSTER, BEEKEEPER

The original Boat Street Café neighbored famed glass artist Dale Chihuly's studio. The staff became friends with the glassblowers, and through them, I met Corky Luster, an endlessly creative man whose résumé includes successful stints in fashion, sculpting, high-end remodeling, and, now, beekeeping. He's thoughtful and charismatic and inappropriate when I need a good laugh most. It feels like we've always been friends.

Corky lives an oddly two-faced life; he spends half the time working in the middle of nowhere with a bunch of stinging insects in the mud, and half the time connecting with chefs and business owners, educating them on how the simple act of supporting honeybees can have a huge impact on our urban environment. He sells a variety of honeys, each made with a particular flavor profile in mind, and also installs personal hives and coaches customers and restaurants on how to keep bees.

Ultimately, Corky is changing the way people make decisions about their food sourcing. He shows customers that with a hive the size of a file cabinet, you can create a valuable food source, but there are also important intangible benefits—bringing back a faltering honeybee population and improving pollination in the community, for example. Corky's hives encourage people to place daily value on their diet, their community, and their environment, which they extrapolate to other things. He makes people learn to think like farmers, developing a vested interest in their food supply and a personal relationship with it.

Corky has been a big part of how my backyard has developed over the years, with flowers and bees instead of just grass. More importantly, my restaurants can serve a product that I feel helps mitigate our inevitable impact on the environment. Today, we have four hives (of the 130 Corky manages) in the Snoqualmie Valley, near Seattle; in a good year, we get forty to fifty pounds of honey from each.

Sundays at Home

Butter Lettuce Salad *123*
Toasted Pistachios, Green Herbs,
Sheep's Milk Cheese

Manila Clams *124*
Spring Onions, Sorrel, Herbs, Crème Fraîche

Grilled Bread *(page 277)*

Roasted Rhubarb *127*
Crème Fraîche Ice Cream

SERVES 4 TO 6

MOST NIGHTS OF THE WEEK, I walk in the door between 10 and 11 p.m. But Sundays, when I make a point of not working at night, I'm usually home before dark. As I open my creaky front gate, Arlo starts to whine from inside the door. I wedge myself past his wiggling dog body, giving him a scratch as I scan the house for signs of his shoe-eating habit, and pour myself a glass of wine.

Between restaurants and friends and family, I do sometimes get burned out on cooking and entertaining for a big crowd. So Sunday night dinners, for me, are simple. I often start by pawing through the condiments in my refrigerator, and find a way to combine the simplest things—a dab of crème fraîche, or a chubby pile of herbs, or a hunk of cheese—with the inevitable bag of something fresh I've picked up on the way home.

In my world, a small dinner is four to six people. On Sunday, cooking for a little group means lots of simple, lighter food, served all at once—in the spring, usually a big salad with whatever my garden grows, shellfish of some sort, and an easy dessert. It's about the people and the wine and the stories of our days, but an excellent pot of clams doesn't hurt.

butter lettuce salad

toasted pistachios, green herbs, sheep's milk cheese

PREP TIME: 15 MINUTES // TOTAL TIME: 15 MINUTES // SERVES 4 TO 6

IN THE SPRING AND SUMMER, WHEN lettuce is prolific and inexpensive, this salad makes the perfect accompaniment to almost anything—chicken, fish, or a simple sandwich. It also has real flavor—something that people don't often associate with butter lettuce.

It's lovely with a simple cocktail made with equal parts dry vermouth and vermouth blanc, balanced with orange bitters and served with a strip of orange peel.

1 cup raw pistachios

1 tablespoon unsalted butter

½ teaspoon flaky sea salt, such as Maldon or Jacobsen (see Resources, page 293), plus more for finishing

Leaves from 2 firm heads butter lettuce (also known as Boston lettuce)

¼ cup torn soft fresh herbs, such as chervil, tarragon, parsley, or chives (ideally a mix of all four)

2 tablespoons freshly squeezed lemon juice (from about 1 medium lemon)

¼ cup grassy extra-virgin olive oil

¼ pound hunk Pecorino Romano cheese

+ Preheat the oven to 350 degrees F.

+ Put the pistachios on a baking sheet and roast for about 10 minutes, or until toasted and fragrant. Immediately transfer the nuts to a small bowl, add the butter and ½ teaspoon of salt, and stir to blend until the butter has melted. Set aside.

+ Pile all the lettuce into a large bowl. Sprinkle the herbs on top, then drizzle with the lemon juice and olive oil, and season with additional salt. Use your hands to toss the lettuce carefully, making sure the herbs and salt are well distributed. Transfer the salad to a large platter and scatter the pistachios on top. Using a very fine grater or Microplane, grate the cheese over the lettuce in a big snowy pile, and serve immediately.

manila clams

spring onions, sorrel, herbs, crème fraîche

PREP TIME: 15 MINUTES // TOTAL TIME: 50 MINUTES, PLUS SOAKING CLAMS
SERVES 4 TO 6

WHEN BOAT STREET CAFÉ'S FIRST LOCATION was forced to close unexpectedly, we moved the brick my dad laid at its entrance to my house. Today, my backyard consists of that giant brick patio, framed by herbs and garden space. Each spring, when the sorrel and chives burst forth, I throw them into a quick clam sauté that relies on crème fraîche for tang and richness.

Spring onions have a lovely green, fresh flavor that's much milder than grown-up onions. If they're tender, use the green tops like herbs, slicing them thinly on the bias and throwing them into the pot right at the end along with the sorrel. In winter, substitute a big handful of chopped thyme or marjoram for the softer spring herbs, adding them with the salt.

Today's shellfish farmers are very good about purging the sand from the clams, but no one likes to eat grit. I clean clams by soaking them in cold water for about half an hour, changing the water two or three times along the way. (If there's still a lot of sand after three changes of water, keep cleaning until no sand remains.)

2 tablespoons extra-virgin olive oil
2 golf ball–size spring onions, peeled, halved, and thinly sliced
¾ cup dry white wine
½ cup heavy cream
1 tablespoon freshly squeezed lemon juice
1 teaspoon kosher salt
5 pounds Manila clams, rinsed

½ cup crème fraîche
1 cup loosely packed, roughly chopped sorrel
¼ cup loosely packed, roughly chopped chervil
¼ cup loosely packed whole tarragon leaves
Freshly ground black pepper
Julienned peel of 1 small lemon

✦ Heat a large, heavy pan over medium heat. Add the oil, then the onions, and cook, stirring, until the onions begin to soften, about 3 minutes. Add the wine, cream, lemon juice, and salt; increase the heat to high; and bring to a boil. Add the clams, cover, and steam for about 5 minutes, or until all the clams have opened.

✦ When the clams have opened (discard any that don't), add the crème fraîche and stir until it melts into the sauce, then add the sorrel, chervil, tarragon, and pepper to taste. Cook for another minute or two, then stir in about two-thirds of the lemon peel. Serve hot, garnished with the remaining lemon peel, with a hunk of bread for dipping.

roasted rhubarb

crème fraîche ice cream

PREP TIME: 10 MINUTES // TOTAL TIME: 55 MINUTES // SERVES 4 TO 6

GROWING UP, WE HAD GIANT RHUBARB plants in the yard, which my mom usually used in strawberry-rhubarb pie. I learned to love its sharp, tart flavor so much that today, I use only the minimum amount of sugar necessary to sweeten it, and instead serve it next to something sweet—in this case, homemade crème fraîche ice cream.

NOTE: The rhubarb can be made ahead and refrigerated, covered, for up to 3 days.

---

1 pound fresh rhubarb
⅔ cups sugar
Pinch kosher salt

Crème Fraîche Ice Cream (recipe follows)

+ With a sharp knife, cut the rhubarb diagonally on a sharp bias into 2-inch-long spears, each about ½ inch thick. (If your rhubarb is exceptionally fat, you may need to cut the spears in half lengthwise first. The goal is to have them close to the same size so they cook evenly.) Place them in a large bowl, toss with the sugar and salt, and let sit for about 30 minutes, so the juices start to come out of the rhubarb. (The sugar will clump up and look sandy.)

+ Preheat the oven to 350 degrees F.

+ Line a baking sheet with parchment paper. One at a time, place the rhubarb on the baking sheet with the cut side down, discarding the extra sugar that winds up in the bottom of the bowl. (It's lovely if you line them all up neatly.) Roast on the oven's middle rack for 8 to 12 minutes, or until the rhubarb is soft when poked with a small, sharp knife but hasn't begun to lose its shape.

+ Remove the rhubarb from the oven and let cool on the baking sheet, then transfer to a bowl along with any juices that collect on the sheet. Serve at room temperature, with the ice cream.

crème fraîche ice cream

PREP TIME: 10 MINUTES // TOTAL TIME: 2 HOURS // MAKES ABOUT 1 QUART
SPECIAL EQUIPMENT: ICE CREAM MAKER

MOST ICE CREAMS REQUIRE A SIGNIFICANT amount of chilling time, but because this one is made by combining warm milk with cold crème fraîche, it comes together quickly. I tend to make it right when I get home, forget about it, and then an hour or two after dinner, remember with a thrill that it's in the freezer.

NOTE: The ice cream will still be soft when it comes out of the machine, so plan to let it chill in the freezer for an hour after you make it.

---

1 cup whole milk
¾ cup plus 1 tablespoon sugar
2½ cups crème fraîche

½ teaspoon vanilla extract
¼ teaspoon kosher salt

✦ In a mixing bowl set over a pot of simmering water, warm the milk and the sugar until the sugar dissolves, stirring occasionally. Remove the bowl from the heat and whisk in the crème fraîche, vanilla, and salt. Cover and refrigerate until chilled, at least 30 minutes.

✦ When cool, freeze the ice cream according to your ice cream maker's instructions, then transfer it to an airtight container and freeze until ready to use, preferably within a day or two.

HOW TO MAKE A CHEESE PLATE

There was a good stretch of my life, when starting a restaurant depleted me of the capacity to cook once I'd left it, when I ate perfect cheese, great bread, and a salad for at least one meal a day. I learned to always ask my cheesemongers what cheeses they love, and more specifically, when to eat the cheeses I chose.

Serving cheese as an appetizer or a course in itself after dinner, I focus on condiments. Bread is great, but serving cheese with ripe seasonal fruit, English oat crackers, or seedy toasts gives good textural contrast and enhances the cheese's flavor.

When you're choosing cheeses, it's important to think about finding a variety of textures. You'll want a combination of ages—a soft fresh cheese, perhaps, next to a harder aged cheese. It's also good to pick a group made with milk from different animals. I try to find cheeses made from local farmers—there are more than forty artisanal cheesemakers in Washington—and focus on tasting the same cheeses throughout the season, as the animals' diet changes.

Below are a few of my favorite pairings:

- *Clothbound cheddar with Honeycrisp or Pippin apples*

- *Tomme de Savoie with Boat Street Pickles' Pickled Apricots (see Resources, page 293)*

- *Ricotta with Sautéed Dates (recipe follows)*

- *Fresh chèvre with stewed cherries*

- *Aged sheep's milk cheese with quince paste*

- *Washed rind cow's milk cheese with roasted walnuts and walnut oil*

- *Bleu cheese with Blackberry Jam with Fresh Bay (page 23) and cracked pepper*

Sautéed Dates

+ Heat ¼ inch sharp extra-virgin olive oil in a small sauté pan over medium heat. Fill the pan with dates and cook, turning them a few times, just until they're warmed through. (They burn easily, so don't overdo it.) Serve them on a plate next to a mound of fresh Ricotta (page 287), with flaky sea salt.

CARRIE OMEGNA, WINE DRINKER

The joke goes like this: Two Burgundian *vignerons* walk into a bar. One is impeccably well groomed, decked out in an Armani suit and beautiful Italian leather shoes. The second is wearing unwashed dungarees and a ripped sweater, and his hands look like dirty roots. Whose wine do you buy?

For me, the answer is obvious. You buy them both, knowing that each wine will taste like the *vignerons* who made them. The first is polished, precise, and focused; the second is earthy, rustic, and honest. Carrie Omegna taught me that.

The way Carrie tells it, I sized her up three times the first day she came in to sell me wine, before even saying hello. I might have been looking at her shoes, or perhaps guessing whether she shared my love for drinkable, low-alcohol French pours.

That was the last time I second-guessed Carrie. From the moment we started tasting bottles together, I knew our approaches matched, that she shared my insistence on pairing food with wines that aren't too overpowering, and that she could teach me as much about wine and the grape-growing process as I'd ever want to know. The third time we met, I invited myself to come with her on a wine-tasting trip to France.

Carrie doesn't want to analyze wine on an academic level; being self-taught makes us both less geeky about pedigree and provenance than our colleagues. She wants to *drink* wine, and over the last decade-plus, she's become my mentor, teaching me how to recognize the difference between wines made in a well-situated vineyard by the guy with the pruning shears and those made in a winery production area.

Carrie has also been instrumental in helping me build my restaurants' wine lists. She spends as much time as I do considering what a wine's relationship will be with food. She allows me to focus on what I like—bright, acidic wines with low tannins, typically neither super juicy nor super dry—but she also helps me balance my favorites with varietals I don't typically gravitate toward. She stretches me.

Carrie and I also agree on one very important thing: if you like a wine, you shouldn't have to justify it. You don't have to like what everyone else likes. You just have to drink it.

SUMMER

Fourth of July Crab Feast

Chilled Melon Soup *139*
Mint, Cayenne, Lime

Boiled Crab *141*
Homemade Mayonnaise

Grilled Crab *142*
Harissa Butter

Grilled Mackerel *145*
Olive Oil, Lemon

Grilled Zucchini *148*
Pickled Cherry Tomato Salad,
Cilantro Vinaigrette

Crab Melts *150*
English Muffins, Tarragon Mayonnaise,
Beecher's Cheddar

Strawberry Shortcake *151*
Cream Biscuits, Sugared Berries

SERVES 6

IN THE STATE OF WASHINGTON, the legal size limit for recreationally caught Dungeness crab is 6¼ inches. Outstretched, my dad's hands measure exactly that from thumbnail to pinky tip. It was convenient to have him around, because when my family crabbed, we never needed the plastic blue measuring device fishermen rely on to determine whether their crab are legal. We just used his hands.

Growing up, crab was as much a part of our Spee-Bi-Dah summers as sand and sun and eighties wedge thong sandals. We crabbed every day we could, boiling them in a giant galvanized pot on the wood stove at night and picking the snowy meat out to provide my mother with a permanent supply, which she kept in a round plastic pie keeper in the refrigerator, loosely covered with a damp paper towel.

We crabbed in a rowboat first, pulling the creatures up in star-shaped traps, then graduated to a nine-foot Livingston boat fitted with a three-horsepower motor. We inevitably got sick of crab—I remember this so clearly—but since we weren't kids with options at dinnertime, we ate Crab Louie, crab melts, crab pasta, crab with crab. What to other families was the ultimate Northwest delicacy was simply a cheap, fun way for us to eat.

Since our kid days, when my brother, Ryan, and I drove our parents mad banging around in our little cabin near the beach, a lot has changed. Now, when Fourth of July rolls around and we gather for our yearly crab feast, Ryan and I drive the boat. If we still carried the crabs up the hill in our orange 5-gallon buckets—"ERICKSON" spray-painted in forest green on the side—we'd be big enough to do it ourselves, but these days, instead of cooking the crabs at the house, we cook them right on the beach, in a pot set over a gas flame.

What I love about Spee-Bi-Dah more than the crab itself is that, because of that sandy beach and the Puget Sound around it, I grew up with a powerful connection to sourcing, cooking, and eating local seafood. Make this menu with food from stores and markets, if you must. But if you're anywhere near the Northwest coast, find a friend with a boat, a crab trap, a shellfish license, and a good beach. Crab really tastes best when you catch it yourself and eat it with friends in front of a sweet summer sunset.

chilled melon soup

mint, cayenne, lime

PREP TIME: 20 MINUTES // TOTAL TIME: 2½ HOURS // SERVES 6

I STARTED MAKING MELON SOUP IN the summers at Boat Street Café, when I needed any excuse not to turn on another heat source in a kitchen with eight burners and two 500-degree ovens. This version, which I make with any ripe summer melon—think Galia, Crenshaw, or Charentais—gets its kick from a pinch of cayenne pepper.

NOTE: When a spoon is inconvenient, as it often is at summer beach parties, serve the soup in little cups.

---

1 (3- to 4-pound) sweet summer melon, such as Galia, Crenshaw, or Charentais
½ cup whole milk yogurt
¼ cup extra-virgin olive oil
Grated zest of ½ large lime
2 tablespoons freshly squeezed lime juice, plus more for seasoning (from about 1 large lime)

4 mint leaves
½ teaspoon flaky sea salt, such as Maldon or Jacobsen (see Resources, page 293), plus more for seasoning
Pinch of cayenne pepper

✦ Seed, peel, and chop the melon into 1-inch pieces, then add it (and any juices you can catch) to the work bowl of a heavy-duty blender or food processor. Add the yogurt, oil, lime zest and juice, mint, salt, and cayenne, and blend until smooth and evenly green. Season to taste with additional lime juice and salt, if necessary. Strain the soup through a fine-mesh strainer, if desired, then chill for 2 hours. Serve cold, in small bowls or cups.

boiled crab

homemade mayonnaise

PREP TIME: 10 MINUTES // TOTAL TIME: 30 MINUTES // SERVES 6

LIKE MANY OF THE FOODS THAT come straight from the ocean, Puget Sound crab tastes best, I find, when it's served at its simplest. On my table, that means simply boiled, with bowls of homemade mayonnaise for dipping.

The most important part of cooking crab is not to overcook it, because the meat gets sticky and dry. If you don't want to cook it yourself, find a fishmonger who will cook it and chill it down for you just before dinner, so you can take it home and eat it fresh.

The belly is my favorite part of the crab, because that's where the meat is sweetest, but we didn't grow up eating the guts, so I don't do it habitually. Eat what you want.

NOTE: If you're buying the crabs instead of catching them and don't have saltwater for cooking, make it by mixing salt into boiling water until it tastes too salty. (Think about what being caught up in the surf at the beach tastes like.)

Kosher salt, for seasoning the
   cooking water
3 (3½-pound) fresh-caught crabs

Homemade Mayonnaise
   (page 280)

✦ Bring a large pot of water to a boil, then add salt until the water tastes like the sea. Add the crabs and cook for 8 minutes, or a minute or two longer if the crabs are substantially larger. Plunge the cooked crabs into an ice bath, let sit until cool, then clean (see Cleaning Crabs, page 143) and serve, with the mayonnaise for dipping.

PICKING DUNGENESS CRAB

I use a cracker to break crab shells apart, but I don't ever use metal crab pickers because the crab itself comes with all the tools you need. Break the smallest joint off one of the crab's claws, and use that to pick the meat out.

grilled crab

harissa butter

PREP TIME: 15 MINUTES // TOTAL TIME: 30 MINUTES // SERVES 6

In Chinese cuisine, pepper crab is a classic dish. This harissa-smeared version—it's important to get the harissa butter on every surface, including inside the belly of the crab—is a similar pairing of flavors, with the hot chili flavor from the harissa melting into the sweet crab flesh. If you can't grill the crabs outdoors, roast them in a 450-degree oven for 5 minutes instead.

And yes, you will get messy. Lick your fingers.

Kosher salt, for seasoning the
    cooking water
3 (3½-pound) fresh-caught crabs

½ cup (1 stick) unsalted butter
¾ cup harissa, such as Rose Petal
    Harissa (page 282)

✦ Bring a large pot of water to a boil, then add salt until the water tastes like the sea. While the water heats, prepare a charcoal or gas grill for cooking over medium-high heat, about 425 degrees F.

✦ Add the crabs to the water and cook for 5 minutes, or a minute or two longer if the crabs are substantially larger or if they have been directly on ice.

✦ Plunge the cooked crabs into an ice bath, let sit until cool, then clean (see Cleaning Crabs, page 143).

✦ While the crabs cool, make the harissa butter: In a small saucepan, melt the butter and harissa together over low heat, stirring occasionally.

✦ Transfer the crabs to a platter and smear them liberally on both sides (and in all their cracks) with the harissa butter. (It's okay if the butter has firmed up a bit.)

✦ Brush the cooking grates clean. Grill the crabs with the lid closed for 2 to 3 minutes, or until the butter has melted into the crevices of each shell, turning once. Serve hot.

CLEANING CRABS

There's nothing particularly sexy about cleaning cooked crabs, but if you catch the things yourself, it has to be done. Luckily, there's no hard and fast rule about the right way to do it; the goal is to get the guts out, pure and simple, so they don't spoil the meat. Here's how my brother, Ryan, does it: He first takes off the back of the crab. Then he breaks the body in half, using his hands to scoop the guts out and pull the gills off the body. He's usually standing shin-deep in saltwater, so he rinses the crab there, but you can just as easily wash away any remaining remnants of the innards in the sink.

grilled mackerel

olive oil, lemon

PREP TIME: 15 MINUTES // TOTAL TIME: 15 MINUTES // SERVES 6

OILY FISH, LIKE MACKEREL, SARDINES, SMELT, and fresh anchovies, are special because their flavor is so intense, but also because they can be cooked in so many ways compared to most white fish. I love them smoked or pickled or straight from a can—silver fish take to canning especially well—and I love them grilled as simply as possible, served with a squeeze of lemon juice.

Don't confine yourself to mackerel here—this dish can also be made with the other oily fish mentioned above. (They're all super healthy and economical, to boot.) Adjust the cooking time accordingly; sardines will take about five minutes to cook and you'll need one or two per person, depending on the fishes' size, and the smaller fish cook very quickly.

3 (1¼-pound) mackerel, heads on
3 lemons, halved
2 tablespoons extra-virgin olive oil
Extra-virgin olive oil, for finishing

Flaky sea salt, such as Maldon or Jacobsen (see Resources, page 293), for finishing

+ Prepare a charcoal or gas grill for cooking over medium-high heat, about 425 degrees F. Smear the fish and the lemons on all sides with the oil.

+ When the grill is hot, brush the cooking grates clean. Grill the mackerel for 8 to 10 minutes with the lid closed, turning once about halfway through when the fish releases easily from the grates, or until just cooked through. Add the lemons to the grill, cut side down, when you turn the fish, and turn them over after about 2 minutes.

+ Transfer the fish and lemons to a platter and serve hot, drizzled with the oil and sprinkled with the salt.

RYAN AND JIM ERICKSON, SUPPORT CREW

I was always a tomboy. I remember the look on my dad's face the first time I gutted a freshly caught salmon—both shocked and proud that daddy's little girl could be so excited about his own passion for fishing.

Part of my enthusiasm was undeniably just competitiveness. My brother, Ryan, two and a half years older, was the classic big brother; he got to do things first, and I always played catch-up. When my dad took him out fishing, crestfallen that I hadn't been included, I'd pout my way down to the water, row out to the dock, and fish by myself, hoping to prove that girls can fish too. Ryan egged me on at every opportunity. He still does, but time has morphed that energy into the sweet, unflagging support I depend on every day. Over the years, he has lifted, moved, and fixed more cantankerous objects than I could possibly list. (He even built me the Cage Mahal of chicken coops.) Ryan has poured his hallmark competitiveness into my goals, and because of it, I'm stronger—and so are my restaurants.

I always had a genuine interest in the activities my family chose, from fishing and crabbing to soccer and baseball. My dad, Jim, was always standing on the sidelines, teaching us to do our best. He paid attention to the details. When I was down, he was up, always rebuilding my ego when something went wrong. He taught me to do something until I get it right. Still today, we talk daily, and he insists on knowing who came into each restaurant and what's new on the menu. My dad carries my business cards and proffers them to total strangers at every opportunity. He's my number one fan.

But more importantly, he and Ryan support me unconditionally, like my whole family has from the day I took over at Boat Street. Without their constant buttressing, I simply wouldn't be in business.

grilled zucchini

pickled cherry tomato salad, cilantro vinaigrette

PREP TIME: 30 MINUTES // TOTAL TIME: 24 HOURS // SERVES 6

ZUCCHINI ARE SIGNIFICANTLY DIFFERENT JUST OFF the vine—they taste greener, and their texture is firmer. Look for the freshest zucchini for this recipe by checking out the stems; the more recently the zucchini has been picked, the less wilted the cut end of the stem will look.

Green coriander, the ripe but not yet dried seed of the cilantro plant, is tough to find; I get it occasionally from Jason and Siri of Local Roots Farm (see Profile, page 179), and it gives a great green, floral flavor without as much astringency as dried coriander seed. If you can find it, add a tablespoon of it to the vinaigrette below.

NOTE: The tomatoes for this salad should be pickled the day before serving.

---

for the PICKLED CHERRY
 TOMATO SALAD:
2 heaping pints red or yellow
 cherry tomatoes, halved
2 cups apple cider vinegar (see
 Resources, page 293)
½ cup sugar
½ teaspoon kosher salt
4 whole tarragon sprigs

for the CILANTRO
 VINAIGRETTE:
1 cup lightly packed fresh cilantro,
 long stems trimmed
1 cup lightly packed fresh Italian
 parsley, long stems trimmed
1 garlic clove, smashed

Grated zest of 1 medium lemon
¼ cup freshly squeezed lemon juice
 (from about 2 medium lemons)
½ teaspoon kosher salt
½ cup extra-virgin olive oil

for the GRILLED
 ZUCCHINI:
6 small zucchini (1½-inch diameter, about 2 pounds total), cut
 into ½-inch-thick slices the
 long way
Extra-virgin olive oil, for brushing
Kosher salt
Flaky sea salt, such as Maldon or
 Jacobsen (see Resources, page
 293), for finishing

✦ First, the day before you plan to serve the salad, pickle the cherry tomatoes: Put the tomatoes in a quart-size jar or a large bowl. In a saucepan, combine the vinegar, sugar, salt, and tarragon, and bring to a boil, stirring until the sugar has dissolved. Pour the hot liquid over the tomatoes, let them cool to room temperature, cover, then refrigerate the tomatoes overnight.

✦ Up to a few hours before serving, make the coriander vinaigrette: In the work bowl of a heavy-duty blender or food processor, buzz the cilantro, parsley, garlic, lemon zest and juice, and salt together until the herbs are very finely chopped.

With the motor running, add the oil in a slow, steady stream through the top of the machine, whirling until the mixture is smooth and bright green. Set aside until ready to use.

✦ Grill the zucchini: Prepare a charcoal or gas grill for cooking over high heat, about 500 degrees F. Brush the zucchini slices liberally on both sides with the oil, then season to taste with the kosher salt.

✦ When the grill is hot, brush the cooking grates clean. Grill the zucchini for 5 to 7 minutes, turning once after the first 3 or 4 minutes, or until the zucchini is marked on both sides and just tender.

✦ Transfer the zucchini to a platter, drizzle with the vinaigrette, and sprinkle with the sea salt. Drain the tomatoes, then pile them on top, and serve the salad warm or at room temperature.

crab melts

english muffins, tarragon mayonnaise,
beecher's cheddar

PREP TIME: 15 MINUTES // TOTAL TIME: 20 MINUTES // MAKES 8

ERASE ALL IDEAS YOU MAY HAVE about adorable seaside sandwiches. Instead, pile toasted English muffins with tall mounds of tarragon-flecked crab salad, douse them with strong cheddar cheese, and broil them until bubbly. This open-faced version of my family's favorite day-after-the-Fourth meal is anything but dainty.

Make these for blunch, in the hour after a bowl of yogurt fails to sustain you but before it's time for lunch.

4 English muffins, such as Thomas'
   brand, split
2 pounds picked crabmeat
½ cup mayonnaise, such as
   Best Foods
⅓ cup chopped fresh tarragon
   leaves

Kosher salt and freshly ground
   black pepper
6 ounces strong white cheddar
   cheese, such as Beecher's
   Flagship (see Resources, page
   293), grated

+ Toast the English muffins until lightly browned in a toaster, and preheat the oven's broiler setting to high.

+ In a large mixing bowl, blend together the crabmeat, mayonnaise, tarragon, and salt and pepper to taste. Place the muffins on a baking sheet, cut sides up. Pile the crab salad onto the muffins, then top the crab with the cheddar.

+ Place the baking sheet on a rack about 4 inches from the broiling unit. Broil the melts with the door partway open until the cheese is melted and bubbly, turning the pan once if needed to melt the cheese evenly, 3 to 5 minutes total. (The meat inside doesn't need to be piping hot.) Serve immediately.

strawberry shortcake
cream biscuits, sugared berries

PREP TIME: 30 MINUTES // TOTAL TIME: 2 HOURS // SERVES 6

MY GODFATHER HAD VERY LARGE TOES. When I saw him as a girl, they always came into view first—huge white things, framed by brown flip-flops. It was those feet, followed usually by his sleeveless jean jacket, a relic from who knows what era, and then him. Jim—my godfather—was an integral part of my summer experience at Spee-Bi-Dah, a beach community about an hour north of Seattle where my family has a cabin.

When I eat shortcake on the beach every Fourth of July, it's hard not to think of those childhood days, and of him. Gather the kids in your life for this recipe, and share it with them as the sun goes down, with plenty of whipped cream and a sparkler. You might be surprised how long they remember the night.

Since the biscuits used here aren't actually sweetened, this same recipe makes delicious savory biscuits; replace the sugar sprinkling on top with a flurry of flaky sea salt.

for the BISCUITS:
2 cups (about 256 grams)
   all-purpose flour
1 tablespoon baking powder
¼ teaspoon baking soda
1 teaspoon kosher salt
¾ cup (1½ sticks) very cold
   unsalted butter, cut into
   ½-inch cubes
1 cup heavy cream
1 tablespoon unsalted butter,
   melted

1 tablespoon demerara sugar
   (see Resources, page 293), for
   topping biscuits

for the STRAWBERRIES:
1 quart strawberries, hulled and
   sliced
2 tablespoons sugar

for the CREAM:
2 cups heavy cream
2 tablespoons sugar

✦ Make the biscuits: In a medium mixing bowl, whisk together the flour, baking powder, baking soda, and salt. Add the butter, breaking it up as you put it in the bowl, then smear the butter into the flour with your fingertips until the mixture is sandy, with a few remaining visible pea-size pieces of butter. Add the cream to the bowl, stirring it in with a wooden spoon until most of the flour is incorporated. Use your hands to knead the dough together a few times, until it comes together.

✦ Turn the dough out onto a floured cool surface. (Stainless steel or marble work well for this.) Pat the dough into a roughly 6-by-6-inch square (about 1 inch thick), then use a floured rolling pin to roll the dough into a long rectangle roughly 6 inches by 18 inches. Cut the dough into thirds, so you have three roughly equal 6-by-6-inch shapes. Stack the layers together, roll a few times in each direction to

continued

make the layers adhere (the dough will get a bit bigger), then wrap the dough in plastic wrap and refrigerate for 30 minutes, or overnight.

✦ Preheat the oven to 425 degrees F. Line a baking sheet with parchment paper and set aside.

✦ Unwrap the dough and use a floured round 2½-inch cutter to cut out six circles. Brush the biscuits with the melted butter, sprinkle with the sugar, and carefully transfer the biscuits to the prepared baking sheet. (You can reroll the remaining dough and repeat the cutting and brushing process, but the biscuits won't be as pretty.)

✦ Bake for 15 to 18 minutes, or until the biscuits are puffed and nicely browned. Let cool for about 30 minutes before serving.

✦ While the biscuits cool, make the berries: In a small mixing bowl, gently blend the berries and sugar together.

✦ Just before serving, make the whipped cream: In the work bowl of a stand mixer fitted with the whisk attachment, whip the cream on medium-high speed for 1 minute. Add the sugar, then whip until the cream forms soft peaks, another minute or two.

✦ To assemble the shortcakes, gently break the biscuits in half horizontally. Place the bottom of each biscuit in a bowl, top with cream and berries, then add the biscuit top. Serve immediately.

Lamb & Rosé Dinner

Two Tartines *158*
Tartine with Chili-Marinated Anchovies and Butter
Ricotta Tartine with Pickled Scapes and Fennel

Pacific Octopus Salad *163*
Grilled Beets, Chermoula, Shaved Fennel and Parsley Salad

Grilled Bread *(page 277)*

Grilled King Salmon *166*
Walnut Tarator, Cherry Tomato Salad

Harissa-Rubbed Roasted Lamb *169*
Yogurt, Olive Oil

Grilled Treviso Radicchio *173*
Anchovy Vinaigrette, Bread Crumbs

Meringues *175*
Apricots, Berries, Cream

SERVES 10

I LOVE ROSÉ. I LOVED IT IN THE BEGINNING, when rosé was first gaining a foothold in the United States, and it's always had a strong presence on my menus. When I became the owner at the original Boat Street Café, I started taking pride in finding rosés that were great food wines—usually bottles from towns in the south of France. I always end up loving the palest pours, especially those made with mourvèdre grapes, because they're rich without being heavy, and they have very little spice to them. In general, rosé stands up to foods that other wines can't, like lamb. Which is why the first summer I owned the restaurant, my employee Russell Flint and I decided to have ourselves a little dinner party.

Part of the frustration of always being behind the stove in a restaurant is that you can't cook everything you want to make to order. Whole roasted chickens require a diner to wait. A grilled leg of lamb is a beautiful piece to behold, but it takes hours to cook, so it's just not a realistic menu item. The Lamb and Rosé Dinner started as a way for us to have fun with close friends, plating things family-style and serving dishes we could never put on our everyday menu. It was an instant hit.

Now, our Lamb and Rosé Dinner takes place annually, each July. It's usually the kind of warm summer evening that brings a whisper of salt air in from the Puget Sound. The cut of lamb changes every year, but some things stay the same: We always cook it on a grate over a fire built in a used wine barrel, the way Russell's grandfather did. We always drink plenty of rosé. And there is always, always dancing.

Because there are many parts to it, this is not the kind of dinner that comes together in an afternoon. At Boat Street Café, we start cooking two or three days in advance (unless you count the chili-marinated anchovies, which are best if they sit for at least a week). It's all done at a rather leisurely pace, much like the celebrations in France it's designed to mimic. It's a menu that requires work, but the path to the party is, in my mind, a crucial part of the experience.

I'm not the type of person who wakes up naturally at the crack of dawn, but my body knows when it's time to open a bottle of rosé. Around 4:30 p.m. on the day of the dinner, after the bulk of the prep work is done (and after the lamb is roasting) but before we need to start plating the tartines, there is a calm, and my inner rosé alarm rings. The waitstaff appear, and the music gets turned up. This, to me, is when the party starts.

Please note that this menu should be served as a dinner party, in the strongest sense of the phrase—a party that happens to include dinner, stretched over the course of hours, not minutes. Although the French don't always eat extravagant, rich foods as they're reputed to, they do almost always take their time.

two tartines

A GOOD *TARTINE*—A FRENCH-STYLE OPEN-FACED SANDWICH—IS the right combination of a well-stocked refrigerator and freshly grilled bread. I like them because they're pretty, and because unlike many sandwiches, which are often too bready for my taste, they have the perfect ratio of stuff.

For each of these tartines, I use the Baguette Toasts on page 278.

tartine with chili-marinated anchovies and butter

PREP TIME: 15 MINUTES // TOTAL TIME: 20 MINUTES, PLUS 1 WEEK
FOR MARINATING ANCHOVIES // MAKES ABOUT 2 DOZEN

I WOULD LOVE IT IF IT were normal for everyone to have a giant can of anchovies in their fridge, like there is in mine. They're a gorgeous way to top tartines for a party—especially marinated in a bright-red chili oil and served over butter shaved with a vegetable peeler or cheese slicer.

That the hot Calabrian chilis I buy are labeled "long" is a bit of a misnomer; they're rarely more than 1½ inches in length. The hot part, though—that's accurate.

Look for a high-quality unsalted butter with a high butterfat content to get the best smooth texture. Brands like Kerrygold, Vermont Creamery, and Crémerie Classique are often available at large natural grocers. Note that it's the balance of butter and spice that makes these tartines so good; skimping on the butter isn't an option.

NOTE: See Resources (page 293) for more information on where to find butter, anchovies, and chilis—it's very important to get good ingredients for this recipe.

---

for the ANCHOVIES:
1 (1.5-pound) can salt-packed
   anchovies (about 60 whole fish,
   bones in), such as Scalia brand
   (see Resources, page 293)
1 (10.2-ounce) jar Calabrian chilis,
   such as Tutto Calabria brand (see
   Resources, page 293)

½ cup extra-virgin olive oil

1 cup (2 sticks) unsalted butter
2 dozen Baguette Toasts
   (page 278)

✦ At least a week before serving the tartines, marinate the anchovies: First soak them according to the instructions in Salts and Salty Things: Anchovies on page 187.

✦ While the anchovies soak, make the oil: Drain the oil from the jar of chilis into the work bowl of a food processor or heavy-duty blender. Add the chilis, removing and discarding the stems (but not the seeds), then pulse the chili oil and chilis together about 10 times, until the chilis are roughly chopped. Add half the chili mixture to a large mixing bowl, then pulse the remaining chilis until very finely chopped but not perfectly pureed. Add the olive oil, and pulse to blend. When the anchovies are dry, transfer them to the bowl, and pour the pureed chili mixture over the them. Using gloved hands, gently blend the anchovies with the chili mixture.

✦ Transfer the anchovies to a large glass container, seal, and refrigerate for at least 1 week, or up to 6 months.

✦ Just before serving, use a cheese slicer, vegetable peeler, or a sharp knife to shave the butter into ⅛-inch-thick slices. Cover each piece of toast with butter shavings (they will look like cheese slices), top each with 2 anchovies, and serve.

ricotta tartine with pickled scapes and fennel

PREP TIME: 30 MINUTES // TOTAL TIME: 30 MINUTES, PLUS OVERNIGHT
FOR PICKLING SCAPES AND FENNEL // MAKES ABOUT 2 DOZEN

GARLIC SCAPES ARE THE CURLICUED SHOOTS that young garlic plants develop in the late spring, before the bulb itself finishes forming in the ground. Scapes have a mellow garlic flavor I love, especially when pickled, blended with sweet young fennel, and piled onto grilled bread smeared with good ricotta.

If you have them on hand, the Pickled Chanterelles (page 218) or Boat Street Café's pickled plums (see Resources, page 293) would work well in place of the scapes and/or fennel. If you prefer to just pickle one thing, make the fennel, then drain and chop it, and blend it with ¼ cup extra-virgin olive oil (along with the finely chopped peel of a preserved lemon, if you want) before topping the ricotta.

NOTE: If you have any of the pickle mixture left when you're finished, toss it into a savory salad, like chicken or tuna salad.

---

for the PICKLED SCAPES:
½ pound garlic scapes (or white
   and light-green parts from
   ¾ pound scallions), cut into
   ¼-inch rounds
2 cups white wine vinegar
2 tablespoons sugar
Julienned peel of 1 medium lemon
1 garlic clove, crushed
½ teaspoon kosher salt
½ cup extra-virgin olive oil

for the PICKLED FENNEL:
4 cups white wine vinegar
¼ cup sugar
5 black peppercorns
3 sprigs fresh thyme

2 fresh bay leaves
½ teaspoon kosher salt
¼ to ½ teaspoon red pepper flakes
¼ cup chopped fresh fennel fronds
   (optional)
1 large or 2 small bulbs fennel
   (about 1 pound total), cored and
   cut into ¼-inch-thick slices

for serving:
2 dozen Baguette Toasts (page 278)
1 pound fresh ricotta cheese
Grassy finishing oil, for drizzling
Flaky sea salt, such as Maldon or
   Jacobsen (see Resources, page
   293), for finishing
½ cup fresh Italian parsley leaves

✦ First, pickle the scapes: In a small saucepan, bring the scapes, vinegar, sugar, lemon peel, garlic, and kosher salt to a simmer over high heat. Reduce the heat to medium and cook for 5 minutes, then remove the pan from the heat and set the scapes aside to cool to room temperature. When cool, transfer the mixture to 2 glass jars. (It's easiest to scoop out the scapes with a slotted spoon and add them first, then to pour the liquid over.) Cover the jars and refrigerate overnight.

✦ Next, pickle the fennel: In a medium saucepan, combine the vinegar, sugar, peppercorns, thyme, bay leaves, kosher salt, red pepper flakes, and fennel fronds. Bring the mixture to a boil, then reduce the heat to a simmer and cook for 5 minutes, stirring occasionally.

✦ Pack the sliced fennel into 3 pint-size glass jars. Carefully pour the hot liquid over the fennel, dividing the herbs and spices between the jars at the end. Cover the jars and refrigerate at least overnight (or up to 1 month).

✦ In the morning, drain the liquid off the pickled scapes and save it for another use (think vinaigrette for a salad), combine all the scapes into one jar, and add the olive oil. (If you want to make the scapes ahead of time, you can store them in the refrigerator in the oil, covered, for up to 2 weeks.)

✦ Drain the pickled fennel, discarding the peppercorns, bay leaves, and thyme. Chop the fennel slices into ¼-inch pieces and transfer them to a small mixing bowl. Pour the pickled scape mixture over the fennel, mixing to coat the fennel with the oil from the scapes.

✦ To serve, smear each piece of toast with a scant tablespoon of ricotta. Top the ricotta with a heaping teaspoon of the pickled scape and fennel mixture, add a pinch of parsley, drizzle with the oil, finish with the sea salt, and serve immediately.

pacific octopus salad

grilled beets, chermoula, shaved fennel
and parsley salad

PREP TIME: 1 HOUR 35 MINUTES // TOTAL TIME: 2 HOURS 30 MINUTES
SERVES 10 AS PART OF A LARGER MEAL, OR 4 TO 6 AS A MAIN COURSE

THIS IS A RECIPE FOR SEATTLEITES, and for Alaskans, but also for anyone willing to step out of their normal pattern of food shopping and find a sustain-
able, trustworthy source for octopus in a place where fishmongers are willing
to think outside the proverbial box. But here's the truth: good octopus caught
in the Pacific Ocean tastes significantly better than the standard baby octopus
you find in most fish markets, which is often caught unsustainably. If you can, I
really want you to cook Pacific octopus. I realize that obtaining it will require a
bit of work. In Seattle, the work involves knowing a fisherman or a fishmonger
and knowing how to ask for just part of one of the giant beasts native to our
local waters.

In our restaurants, we have access to giant Pacifics—they sometimes weigh
thirty-five pounds apiece—which we cut and cook many different ways. (Try the
octopus terrine at Barnacle.) For this recipe, we use two cooking methods. First,
we cut the head and wrist-thick tentacles into hunks and braise them in a mixture
of aromatics and wine until absolutely tender, when the big pieces measure about
120 degrees F on a thermometer.

Next, we cook the small, winding tentacles in pieces in olive oil, with just
lemon peel, bay leaf, and the water the octopus stores up in its own cells. Since
the smaller pieces become tender much more quickly than the larger ones, this
allows us to cook each piece perfectly.

In my dream world, you'd do the same thing; you'd find just a leg or two of
a big guy and cook it two separate ways. I know, though, that it'll probably be
easiest for you to buy two smaller octopuses (or four tiny ones, if that's all you
can find), so that's what I've called for in the recipe below. The smaller ones cook
well using the second method. (If you buy frozen octopus, thaw it slowly and
completely in the refrigerator for two or three days before cooking.) Look for
wild-caught Pacific octopus from California, Hawaii, or Alaska—or, as we do,
ask a fisherman to set aside his by-catch for you.

If you've never cooked octopus before, don't worry—it's much sexier to eat
than it is to look at when it's raw.

To save time the day you serve the salad, boil the beets and make the chermoula a day or two ahead, and assemble the fennel and parsley salad at the very
last minute.

continued

for the BEETS:
1 tablespoon kosher salt, plus more
    for seasoning
1½ pounds golden beets (about
    4 medium), greens trimmed
1½ pounds red beets (about
    4 medium), greens trimmed
¼ cup extra-virgin olive oil
1 cup Chermoula (page 284)

for the OCTOPUS:
½ cup extra-virgin olive oil
5 cloves garlic, smashed
Stripped peel of ½ large lemon
2 (4-pound) raw octopuses,
    cleaned, rinsed, and drained (see
    Resources, page 293)
1 tablespoon sea salt

2 fresh bay leaves
¼ cup extra-virgin olive oil
Kosher salt

for the SALAD:
1 large or 2 small bulbs fennel
    (about 1 pound total)
5 tablespoons freshly squeezed
    lemon juice (from about 2 large
    lemons), divided
2 loosely packed cups fresh Italian
    parsley leaves
¼ cup extra-virgin olive oil, plus
    more for drizzling salad
Kosher salt, for finishing
Flaky sea salt, such as Maldon or
    Jacobsen (see Resources, page
    293), for finishing

✦ First, cook the beets: In a large saucepan, bring about 8 cups of water to a boil. Add the kosher salt, then all the beets, and cook until a skewer inserted into the center of each beet comes out without resistance, about 1 hour. Drain the beets and set them aside until they are cool enough to handle.

✦ When the beets have cooled, trim the tough top off each beet, slip the skins off (reserving the root tails, if possible), and cut each beet into 6 or 8 wedges, depending on the size. Set the wedges aside to cool completely. (If you are making the beets ahead, transfer the sliced beets to a covered container and refrigerate them for up to 3 days.)

✦ While the beets cook, make the octopus: In a large, round soup pot, combine the olive oil, garlic, and lemon peel and cook over low heat until the garlic begins to soften and brown a bit, about 5 minutes, turning and stirring occasionally.

✦ Meanwhile, cut the octopus into sections, cutting the tentacles off where they meet the bodies, and cutting each of the bodies into 4-inch strips. Add the octopus pieces, sea salt, and bay leaves to the pot, and stir to coat the octopus in the oil. Place a plate just smaller than the diameter of the pot directly onto the octopus to prevent it from bobbing around. Bring the liquid back to a gentle simmer, then cook for 30 minutes over low heat, stirring the octopus once or twice. Remove the plate to see how much liquid the octopus has produced; if it seems like less than about a cup, add a cup of water to the pot. Return the plate to the octopus, bring the liquid back to a boil, and simmer another 30 to 60 minutes, checking the octopus tentacles and head pieces for tenderness with a skewer every few minutes after a total of 1 hour cooking time. (It should be obvious when the octopus becomes tender; it tends to happen all at once, and the octopus shrinks considerably.) Remove the pot from the heat and let the octopuses cool in the liquid. (Cover and refrigerate up to a day ahead, if desired.)

+ When the octopuses have cooled, remove them from the liquid and strip the pieces of their slick black coating, if necessary. Cut the tentacles and body pieces diagonally into 2-inch sections (each about the size of 2 bites). Transfer the sections to a bowl, and set them aside.

+ A few hours before serving, prepare the salad ingredients: Core the fennel, shave it into paper-thin slices on a mandoline, and toss it with about 3 tablespoons of the lemon juice. Refrigerate the fennel until you assemble the salad.

+ Up to 3 hours before serving (or immediately before), grill the beets and octopus: Preheat a charcoal or gas grill for cooking over high heat, about 500 degrees F.

+ Drain any excess liquid off the beets and toss them with the olive oil, then season to taste with kosher salt. Brush the cooking grates clean. Grill the beets for about 10 minutes, covered, turning once or twice during cooking, or until the beets are well marked on all sides. Transfer the beets to a large bowl and set aside.

+ Next, toss the octopus pieces with the olive oil and season to taste with kosher salt. Make sure the grill has come back up to temperature, then grill the octopus over high heat, taking care not to lose the pieces between the grates, for 2 to 3 minutes, just until charred, turning once. Set aside to cool.

+ To serve, blend the beets with the chermoula and place the beets on the bottom of a large platter (or on individual plates). In a large bowl, toss together the grilled octopus, fennel, parsley, the remaining 2 tablespoons of the lemon juice, the olive oil, and kosher salt to taste. Place the salad on top of the beets, drizzle with additional olive oil, and sprinkle with the sea salt. Serve immediately.

grilled king salmon

walnut tarator, cherry tomato salad

PREP TIME: 45 MINUTES // TOTAL TIME: 1 HOUR 25 MINUTES
SERVES 10 AS PART OF A LARGER MEAL, OR 6 AS A MAIN COURSE

BEFORE WE GRILL THE LAMB OVER a barrel at the Lamb and Rosé Dinner, we always grill fatty salmon, accompanied here by *tarator*, a traditional Balkan or Middle Eastern dish that comes in as many variations as hummus. This yogurt-free variation, made with walnuts, bread, and olive oil, makes an excellent sauce. At Boat Street Café, we also make it with hazelnuts occasionally.

In July, we usually get gorgeous marbled king salmon, known for its rich flesh, but you can also use regular king salmon, or sockeye—just adjust the cooking time as necessary, because thinner fillets will take less time.

NOTE: If you buy a whole salmon that needs scaling, place the fish in a clear plastic garbage bag, and scale the fish with the back of a small, sharp knife *inside* the garbage bag, scraping the back of the blade from tail to head to remove the scales without making a huge mess.

---

for the SALMON:
1 (3½- to 4-pound) king salmon fillet, roughly 2 to 2½ inches thick in the center
1 tablespoon extra-virgin olive oil
Kosher salt, for seasoning
Finishing oil, for drizzling
Flaky sea salt, such as Maldon or Jacobsen (see Resources, page 293), for finishing

for the TARATOR:
2 cups whole walnuts, toasted (see Toasting Nuts, page 12)
1 cup 1-inch cubes baguette or other artisanal bread (including the crust)
½ cup freshly squeezed lemon juice (from about 4 medium lemons)

1 clove garlic, smashed
1 teaspoon kosher salt
1 cup water
1 cup extra-virgin olive oil

for the SALAD:
2 pints summer cherry tomatoes, halved
1 pound lemon cucumbers (or English cucumbers), cut into ½-inch cubes
¼ cup roughly chopped fresh dill
Julienned peel and juice of 1 large lemon
¼ cup extra-virgin olive oil
Flaky sea salt, such as Maldon or Jacobsen (see Resources, page 293), for finishing

✦ Make the salmon: Preheat a charcoal or gas grill for cooking over medium heat, about 375 degrees F. Brush the salmon with the olive oil, then season it to taste with kosher salt. Brush the cooking grates clean. Grill the salmon (without turning) until just cooked through at the ends (but still a bit translucent in the center), keeping the lid closed, about 30 minutes for fish 2 to 2½ inches thick at the fattest part. (You can grill the salmon just before serving and serve it warm, but I actually prefer to grill it a bit ahead of time and serve it at room temperature.)

✦ Meanwhile, make the tarator: Place the walnuts, bread cubes, lemon juice, garlic, and kosher salt in the work bowl of a food processor or a heavy-duty blender. Pour the water over the bread, pulse a few times to mix, then whirl on high speed until smooth, adding the oil in a slow, steady stream through the top of the machine with the motor running. Spread the tarator out in a puddle on a large platter and set aside. (The tarator can also be made ahead, refrigerated for up to 3 days, and allowed to come back to room temperature before serving.)

✦ Make the salad: In a large mixing bowl, combine the tomatoes, cucumbers, dill, lemon peel and juice, and olive oil. Season to taste with the kosher salt.

✦ When the salmon is done, break it apart into serving-size hunks and arrange them on the tarator. Spoon the salad over the salmon, followed by a drizzle of olive oil and a shower of sea salt. Serve at room temperature.

harissa-rubbed roasted lamb

yogurt, olive oil

PREP TIME: 15 MINUTES // TOTAL TIME: 3 HOURS, PLUS MARINATING
SERVES 8 TO 10
SPECIAL EQUIPMENT: 7 (3-FOOT-LONG) PIECES KITCHEN STRING

IN THE SOUTHWESTERN PART OF FRANCE, the Moroccan impact on cuisine is similar to that of Mexican cooking in the southwestern United States. We forget, as Americans used to our own amalgam of culinary cultures but happy to pigeonhole others', that so-called French cooking extends far beyond coq au vin and lyonnaise salad. This lamb is as French as those more well-known dishes.

At Boat Street Café, we cook the lamb over an old wine barrel converted into a grill until it's well charred on the outside, then finish it in the kitchen's oven. The lamb comes out a good hour or so before it's actually served, so that we can plate the other courses and welcome guests without worrying about it. (It also tastes delicious at room temperature.) If you prefer, you can cook the lamb on a gas or charcoal grill from start to finish—lamb has a richness that makes it taste really delicious cooked over a fire. Just do your best to keep your grill temperature at about 375 degrees F for the latter part of the cooking process.

NOTE: If you're up for a challenge, tie the lamb using a real butcher's knot. Rain Shadow Meats' Russell Flint taught me how to make them years ago, and I find them quite practical. Otherwise, tie your lamb any which way—the point is simply to keep the meat together.

---

1 (6- to 7-pound) boneless lamb leg	1 tablespoon kosher salt
1 cup harissa, such as Rose Petal Harissa (page 282)	2 cups Homemade Yogurt (page 286)
	Extra-virgin olive oil, for finishing

✦ A day or two before you plan to cook the lamb, marinate it in the harissa: First, open the lamb leg on a cutting board. Feel around the interior of the meat for any little knobs or nodules; a good butcher will cut out the hard gland (actually a lymph node) behind the lamb's knee, but if yours hasn't, remove it with a small, sharp knife. Leave the fat cap that lines the top of the leg.

✦ Smear the harissa on all sides of the lamb. Using 3-foot-long pieces of kitchen string, tie the lamb together into a tubular shape, placing the string at regular intervals. (I like to tie the ends first, then the middle, then put string between the middle and the ends, incorporating any meat sections that want to poke out.) Place the lamb in a baking dish and refrigerate, covered, for 1 to 3 days.

continued

➤ Before cooking, remove the lamb from the refrigerator and let it come to room temperature for about 1 hour. Sprinkle the salt over the lamb on all sides.

➤ Preheat a charcoal or gas grill for cooking over medium-high heat, about 425 degrees F. Preheat the oven to 375 degrees F as well.

➤ Brush the cooking grates clean. Grill the lamb, fat side down first, for about 15 minutes, turning occasionally (the edges may char, but that's okay). When the lamb is well browned, transfer it to a roasting pan and roast it in the oven until the thickest part of the leg measures 120 degrees F on an instant-read thermometer for rare (or 125 degrees F for medium), about 1 hour 15 minutes. (Note that the meat will continue cooking for a good 15 minutes after it comes out of the oven, so it's important to pull it out before the inside is actually done cooking.)

➤ Let the meat rest for at least 30 minutes, or up to 2 hours, before slicing it into ½-inch-thick pieces. To serve, smear the yogurt onto a platter and arrange the lamb slices on top. Drizzle with the oil.

MY FAVORITE ROSÉS

Most rosés are intended to be sipped within a year of their release. Here's a good blend of bottles I love, with a wide variety of price points.

- *Château d'Or et de Gueules, Costières de Nîmes*

- *Clos Canarelli, Corsica*

- *Clos Sainte-Magdeleine, Cassis*

- *Domaine du Gros 'Noré, Bandol*

- *Domaine Hippolyte Reverdy, Sancerre*

MY NEW LOVE

I have a new crush: Corsican rosé. Born from the dry mountains of Corsica, the French island south of the Continent, Corsican wines have a unique pedigree because they blend relatives of Italian grape varietals, such as Nielluccio and Sciaccarellu, with French wine-making traditions. (Corsica belonged to the Republic of Genoa, now part of Italy, until the French took it over in the eighteenth century.) The island's cool marine nights give the grapes great minerality and gentle floral flavors, often with melon notes. Overall, the wines have a softer fruity flavor, with more peach pit notes, than the typical ripe-strawberry profile people tend to assign to rosé.

In general, I think the best way to decide what to eat with a given wine is to examine the cuisine of the culture that's been drinking it for generations. On Corsica, the population is more of a mountainous culture, despite its bountiful shorelines, and its rosés pair best with what people eat there—interesting sheep's milk cheeses, hot-weather fruit like figs and apricots, and meats like pork and lamb.

grilled treviso radicchio

anchovy vinaigrette, bread crumbs

PREP TIME: 20 MINUTES // TOTAL TIME: 45 MINUTES // SERVES 8 TO 10

BEFORE THESE TORPEDO-SHAPED BITTER GREENS ARE cut, oiled, and grilled, they're stunning to look at—the Treviso radicchio we get from Local Roots Farm (see Profile, page 179) has pale-green centers and royal-purple leaves. It's those gorgeous colors, I think, that give cooks pause when they're grilling, but it's crucial to give these greens a good char when you're preparing them.

The last time I made grilled Treviso for the Lamb and Rosé Dinner, I was cooking with chef Jay Guerrero, who sometimes claims to be half Black Irish, half Mexican, and half cowboy. It's a big fat lie, but no one would argue that he has a killer singing voice, especially if he happens to be standing in Boat Street Café's blazing hot kitchen on a summer day with the grill on full blast.

5 heads Treviso raddichio
¼ cup extra-virgin olive oil
Kosher salt

Anchovy Vinaigrette (recipe follows)
½ cup Homemade Bread Crumbs (page 276)

✦ Preheat a charcoal or gas grill for cooking over medium-high heat, about 425 degrees F.

✦ Trim a tiny bit off the ends of each raddichio head, so the brown part is gone but the heads are still totally intact, then halve them lengthwise (or quarter them, if they seem especially large). Brush the halves on both sides with the olive oil, then season to taste with salt.

✦ Brush the cooking grates clean. Add the radicchios and grill for 4 to 6 minutes total, until well charred, moving them as little as possible. They should be soft on the outside but still a bit firm in the centers; you may need to cook the root ends of each radicchio a bit more (with the tips on the cooler part of the grill) if they seem too firm to cut with a table knife.

✦ Transfer the radicchios to a large platter, lining them up parallel to each other, and let cool to room temperature. Just before serving, drape the radicchios with the anchovy vinaigrette (to taste) and sprinkle them with the bread crumbs.

anchovy vinaigrette

PREP TIME: 15 MINUTES // TOTAL TIME: 15 MINUTES,
PLUS TIME TO SOAK ANCHOVIES // MAKES: ABOUT 1½ CUPS

IT'S ONE THING TO HAVE ANCHOVIES in a salad dressing—they add great depth—
but another thing entirely to make anchovy vinaigrette. Here's an unabashed
version that relies on the whole anchovies for color and plenty of flavor.

For instructions on how to debone whole anchovies and soak salt-packed
anchovies before using, see Salts and Salty Things: Anchovies on page 187.

15 whole salt-packed anchovies,
soaked and bones removed, or
30 oil-packed anchovy fillets
(see Resources, page 293)
Grated zest of 1 large lemon
¼ cup freshly squeezed lemon juice
(from about 2 medium lemons)

1 large garlic clove, smashed
½ teaspoon kosher salt
⅛ teaspoon freshly ground black
pepper
½ cup extra-virgin olive oil

✦ In the work bowl of a food processor or heavy-duty blender, puree the anchovies, lemon zest and juice, garlic, salt, and pepper until completely smooth. With
the motor running, add the oil in a slow, steady stream through the top of the
machine, processing until the oil is fully incorporated and the vinaigrette is very
smooth and creamy. Use immediately, or refrigerate, covered, for up to 3 days.

SETTING THE TABLE

Be prepared to break out more than your day-to-day dishware for this
menu. Although none of the dishes are that complicated on their own,
there are many of them, and the flavors don't translate well from recipe to
recipe—so instead of inviting your guests to mop up spicy *chermoula* with
their delicate salmon, plan on giving them new plates for each course. At
the restaurant, our plates match, but at home, I'm content to mix plate sets
with orphan plates as long as the general style is the same.

Flowers are an integral part of the Lamb and Rosé Dinner as well,
but each year, they change. In general, I pick my flowers based on what
the table needs and what the weather requires. In the case of Boat Street
Café, that means something casual and simple, because it matches the
atmosphere. If it's a cool evening, I'll bring hydrangeas from my garden,
because, like our region's salmon, they're often at their peak in mid-July.
If it's sweltering, I'll pick sunflowers, because they stand up well to the
heat. Listen to your garden. It will tell you what to do.

meringues

apricots, berries, cream

PREP TIME: 15 MINUTES // TOTAL TIME: 3 TO 4 HOURS // MAKES 1 DOZEN

THERE'S NO WAY AROUND IT: I love meringue. Every time I scoop the pearly batter into my mouth raw, just after turning off the mixer, I hear my mother's voice in the back of my head. "You're going to get *sick*," she promises. Somehow, I never do. Chalk it up to luck if you want; I attribute my fortune to using eggs from happy chickens. I suggest you do the same, so that when you're done plopping huge scoops of meringue onto a parchment-covered baking sheet, you can lick your fingers with zero hesitation.

But let's get something straight: I'm no baker. Over the years, I've developed the simplest recipe I know of, using equal parts egg white and sugar by weight, plus a pinch of salt. (If you have a scale, measure your egg whites before straining them, and use the same weight in sugar, instead of the measurements given below.) There's no vanilla to mask the flavor of a fresh egg, and there's no cream of tartar—just a poufy kiss of shattery meringue, perfect topped with sweetened fruit and a bit of cream. If you're putting a dessert into the oven, it doesn't get much simpler.

I personally don't worry much about meringues weeping. Occasionally—especially on particularly hot or humid days, or if I forget to use the oven's convection setting, or if I'm out of superfine sugar and just make do with regular sugar—mine do, and I revel in the caramel the sugar forms underneath the meringues. Eat them anyway.

NOTE: To warm eggs to room temperature quickly, place them in a bowl with enough warm water to cover and let them sit on the counter for about 10 minutes. It's important to do this; cold egg whites won't whip up as well as room-temperature whites.

---

for the MERINGUES:
8 large egg whites (about 265g),
   at room temperature
⅛ teaspoon kosher salt
1⅓ cups (265g) superfine sugar

for the TOPPING:
12 ripe apricots, halved or quartered if larger than a walnut, and pitted
¼ cup granulated sugar, divided
2 pints raspberries or blackberries, or a mixture of both
1 cup heavy cream
1 tablespoon light brown sugar

continued

✦ Make the meringues: Preheat the oven to 200 degrees F on the convection bake setting. Line 2 baking sheets with parchment paper and set them aside.

✦ Strain the egg whites through a fine-mesh strainer to rid them of their small white flecks (called chalazae). It may take a minute or two; gather as much patience as you can muster and use a rubber scraper to push the whites through the strainer.

✦ In the work bowl of a stand mixer fitted with the whisk attachment (make sure that both the bowl and whisk are clean and dry), whip the whites on medium speed until frothy. Add the salt; then, with the mixer still running, add the sugar in a slow, steady stream. When all of the sugar has been added, increase the speed to high and whip for 5 minutes, until the mixture forms stiff peaks and has a pearly sheen to it. If you rub a bit of the mixture between two fingers, you should no longer feel little sugar granules. (I strongly believe that in this state, meringue is one of the world's most beautiful foods.)

✦ Using 2 large serving spoons, drop the mixture in orange-size blobs onto the prepared baking sheets, about 6 per sheet, pushing one spoon into the middle of each to form a well, which will be filled with fruit later. (Each meringue should measure about 4 inches across, with a roughly 2-inch-wide well.) Expect the batter to bend and smear differently for each meringue; it's okay if strands of the batter stick out at quirky angles.

✦ Bake the meringues for 3 hours, or until they are dry and crackly on the outside and still just a bit moist in the center—similar to a marshmallow, but not at all spreadable. Remove the meringues from the oven and let cool completely on the baking sheets before using, or, if you prefer slightly drier meringues, return the meringues to the oven, turn the oven off, and let the meringues dry out in the oven overnight.

✦ Make the topping: About 30 minutes before serving, stir the apricots together with 2 tablespoons of the sugar in one bowl, and the berries together with the remaining 2 tablespoons of the sugar in another bowl.

✦ In the work bowl of a stand mixer fitted with the whisk attachment, whip the cream on medium-high speed for 1 minute. Add the brown sugar, then whip until the cream forms soft peaks, another minute or two.

✦ To serve, place the meringues on small plates. Fill the wells with whipped cream, top with the apricots and berries, and serve immediately.

JASON SALVO AND SIRI ERICKSON-BROWN, LOCAL ROOTS FARM

If there's such a thing as a farming fairy tale, it takes place in Duvall, WA, where junior high sweethearts Jason Salvo and Siri Erickson-Brown of Local Roots Farm have put down roots of all kinds. Both born to families where farming runs deep, the couple didn't start on the land, but traveling to work on a farm in Italy before returning to Washington for graduate school (for degrees in law and public policy, respectively) instilled in them an infectious enthusiasm for growing the best produce possible.

Local Roots Farm was so named because Jason and Siri had mothers who graduated from a Seattle high school together and both had families that had historically sold produce. It started as a six-acre experiment. At first, Jason supplemented their income with another job. They realized that if they wanted to have a family, they'd need to rely less on nonstop work and more on scaling up their production levels. In 2011, after the birth of their son, Felix, they bought eighty acres of gorgeous farmland just northeast of Seattle.

Today, the couple—and now their young family—is known in the Seattle area for growing the best Italian specialties, like broccoli rabe, Treviso radicchio, artichokes, purslane, and spigarello. Gorgeous greens arrive at my restaurants in boxes that make me feel like a kid at Christmas. (It doesn't hurt that Jason often adorns the boxes with boats, whales, or walruses, depending on their destinations.)

I love that Jason and Siri know how to focus on what they're great at growing. I love that they listen to me, and now instinctively know what I'll want for my restaurants. I love that they'll carefully winter over delicious vegetables I can take pride in serving in January and February. And I love that as they grow, I can trust that they'll continue to farm with the same mindful care they've used since the beginning.

❧ SUMMER INGREDIENTS ❧

BLACKBERRIES

Blackberry Cobbler

✦ Follow the recipe for Peach Cobbler (page 202), substituting **6 pints blackberries** for the peaches. *Serves 8 to 10.*

Blackberry Eton Mess

✦ In a mixing bowl, combine **2 pints blackberries** with **2 tablespoons sugar** and let sit for 30 minutes, until the blackberries give up their juices. Break **3 Meringues** (page 175) into various-size pieces. Whip **1 pint heavy cream** into soft peaks, adding **1 tablespoon brown sugar** near the end of whipping. Divide half the whipped cream between four shallow bowls. Top the cream with half the meringue pieces and half the berries, then repeat, layering in cream and meringue and finishing with the remaining berries and juice. *Serves 4.*

Red Wine–Blackberry Syrup

✦ In a large saucepan, combine **2 pints blackberries** with **1½ cups dry red wine, 1 cup sugar,** and **1 sprig fresh thyme.** Bring the mixture to a strong simmer over medium heat and cook for about 45 minutes, stirring occasionally, until it begins to thicken and has reduced to about 4 cups. Transfer to a quart-size jar to cool. Serve the syrup with the **crêpes** from the Gâteau de Crêpes (page 78), either simply drizzled on top or over the crêpes rolled around mounds of fresh ricotta (see the recipe on page 287). *Makes 4 cups.*

MELON

Watermelon Panzanella

✦ In a large bowl, combine **4 cups toasted 1-inch bread cubes** (from about 4 big slices of Grilled Bread, page 277) with **4 cups cubed watermelon** (from half a 5-pound seedless melon), and toss with **4 ounces crumbled feta cheese, ½ cup torn fresh mint leaves, ¼ cup freshly squeezed lime juice, ½ cup extra-virgin olive oil,** and **kosher salt and pepper** to taste. *Serves 4.*

Cantaloupe and Ice Cream

✦ It's a kid's favorite, but it's one of mine too: Halve a **small cantaloupe or Charentais melon** and scrape out the seeds. Add a big scoop of **vanilla ice cream** to the centers and dig in with a spoon. *Serves 2.*

Charentais Melon Sorbet

✦ Make a sugar syrup by simmering **2 cups sugar** and **1 cup water** together in a small saucepan until the sugar dissolves completely. Transfer the syrup to a jar and chill until cold. Chop the flesh of **half a 4-pound Charentais melon** (or cantaloupe) and blend with **¾ cup Moscato d'Asti** until smooth. Add the sugar syrup to the melon mixture, mix just to blend, and freeze in an ice cream maker according to manufacturer's instructions. *Makes 1 quart.*

PEPPERS

Fresh Pepper Pipérade

✦ First, roast **2 large red peppers:** Char the peppers over a gas flame or a hot grill until black and blistered all over. Let cool in a sealed paper bag, then peel, seed, and thinly slice the peppers. In a large skillet, heat **2 tablespoons extra-virgin olive oil.** Add **1 sliced small onion** and **2 sliced large garlic cloves,** and cook, stirring, until soft, about 10 minutes. Add **1 heaping cup julienned roasted red peppers,** **¼ cup sherry vinegar,** **2 tablespoons more olive oil, 2 teaspoons smoked Spanish paprika,** and **1 teaspoon kosher salt,** and reduce the heat to low. Cook the mixture for another 45 minutes, until the onions are golden and most of the liquid has disappeared. Season to taste with salt. Serve with grilled fish or smeared onto a plate, with a poached egg on top. *Makes about 2 cups.*

Roasted Red Pepper Flan

✦ Here's an old-school Boat Street Café favorite: Whisk together **4 large eggs** and **3 cups heavy cream** until frothy. Whisk in **1 cup finely grated Parmesan cheese, 1 teaspoon Dijon mustard, 1 teaspoon kosher salt,** and a fresh grating of **nutmeg.** Stuff an 8-cup baking dish (or two 4-cup dishes) with **½ pound baby spinach,** top with **½ cup roasted red or *piquillo* peppers** (see above) cut into ½-inch strips, then scatter **3 ounces crumbled goat cheese** on top. Carefully pour half the egg mixture over the vegetables,

continued

then scatter **1 tablespoon tarragon leaves** on top. Repeat, piling another entire **½ pound spinach** on top (you'll have to stack the leaves to sneak them in), then another **½ cup sliced peppers**, **3 ounces goat cheese**, and **1 tablespoon tarragon leaves**. Place the dish(es) on a baking sheet, then carefully pour in the remaining egg mixture. Bake at 400 degrees F for about 1 hour, or until the custard has puffed, the top is browned and crusty, and the egg is firm in the center. Shower with flaky sea salt and serve immediately, with good bread. (Note that the eggs will curdle a bit; this is normal.) *Serves 4.*

Sautéed Padrón Peppers

✤ Heat a large, heavy skillet over high heat. When the pan is hot, add **2 tablespoons extra-virgin olive oil**, then **½ pound Padrón peppers** (see Resources, page 293). Season the peppers generously with crunchy **sea salt**. Let the peppers cook for about 3 minutes, turning each once or twice during cooking, until they are charred on all sides. You'll know the peppers are done when they're very deep brown and begin "breathing" in the pan, puffing in and out as they cook. Transfer the peppers to a platter and serve, showered with additional sea salt. *Serves 4.*

TOMATOES

Fresh Corn and Tomato Salad

✤ Combine **1 pint halved Sungold tomatoes** with raw kernels from **2 fresh corn cobs** in a large bowl. Add **½ cup loosely packed green herbs** (such as basil, tarragon, chervil, and/or parsley), **¼ cup finely chopped red onion**, **¼ cup extra-virgin olive oil**, the **juice of 1 medium lemon**, and **salt and pepper** to taste. Mix well. *Serves 4.*

Fresh Tomato Pasta

✤ In a large skillet, warm **¼ cup extra-virgin olive oil** over medium heat along with **2 cloves' worth of thinly sliced garlic**. When the garlic begins to sizzle, grate **3 large beefsteak tomatoes** into the oil. (You can finely chop them instead, if you prefer.) Season the tomatoes with **salt and pepper** and cook, stirring, for about 5 minutes. Meanwhile, cook **½ pound spaghetti** al dente according to package instructions in well-salted water. Drain the pasta, mix it with the tomatoes, and serve piping hot, with torn **basil** and a snowy pile of a **Pecorino Romano** cheese. *Serves 2.*

My Favorite Summer Sandwich

✦ Slather **Grilled Bread** (page 277) with **mayonnaise**. Stack with thick-sliced **beefsteak tomatoes**, season with **flaky sea salt** and **cracked black pepper**, and eat with both hands. *Serves 1.*

ZUCCHINI

Sausage-Stuffed Zucchini

✦ Trim and discard the top thirds of **4 round Eight Ball zucchini** (about 1½ pounds). Scoop out the insides with a spoon or melon baller, leaving roughly ½ inch of flesh all around, and finely chop the scooped zucchini. Sauté the chopped zucchini over medium heat in **2 tablespoons olive oil** until tender, then season with **kosher salt and pepper** and transfer to a bowl. Stir in **⅓ pound cooked, crumbled Italian sausage, ¾ cup cooked couscous, ½ cup crumbled feta, ¼ cup chopped fresh Italian parsley, ¼ cup golden raisins, 2 tablespoons heavy cream,** and **2 tablespoons toasted pine nuts.** Season the mixture to taste with more kosher salt and pepper, then pile it back into the zucchini. Top the stuffing with **¼ cup Bread Crumbs** (page 276) and drizzle with **2 more tablespoons olive oil**, then bake at 400 degrees F until the zucchini are soft and the tops are golden brown, about 20 minutes. *Serves 4.*

Shaved Zucchini Salad

✦ Shave **1 pound raw unpeeled zucchini** into paper-thin ribbons lengthwise on a mandoline (or with a vegetable peeler), then toss with **½ cup Mint and Parsley Pesto** (from the Raw Asparagus Salad recipe on page 116) and **2 tablespoons toasted pine nuts.** Serve topped with another **2 tablespoons toasted pine nuts**, a drizzle of **extra-virgin olive oil**, and a sprinkle of crunchy **sea salt**. *Serves 2 to 4.*

Zucchini Gratin

✦ Mix **1 pound grated zucchini** with **1 teaspoon kosher salt** in a colander and let sit for 15 minutes. Squeeze the zucchini between your hands over the sink to remove excess water, blot with paper towels, and spread out in an 8-inch baking pan. Season with **½ teaspoon more kosher salt**, freshly ground **black pepper** and freshly grated **nutmeg** to taste, and **2 tablespoons roughly chopped tarragon leaves.** Pour **½ cup heavy cream** evenly over the zucchini, top with **¼ pound grated Gruyère cheese**, and bake for about 30 minutes at 400 degrees F, until browned and bubbling. *Serves 4.*

My Birthday

Radishes *191*
Green Goddess Dressing

Marinated Olives *192*
Thyme, Garlic, Lemon Peel

Grilled Dry-Aged Rib-Eye Steaks *195*
Anchovy Butter

Tomatoes *197*
Olive Oil, Vanilla Bean Salt

Potato Salad *201*
Preserved Lemon, Chives

Peach Cobbler *202*

SERVES 8

I LIKE TO JOKE THAT MY BIRTHDAY is a national holiday, because that's the way I treat it. But it's not my fault. From the time I was very young, my parents celebrated August 10 with an energy and intensity I now recognize as rare. We used to have giant backyard parties with croquet and badminton and barbecue, and make homemade strawberry ice cream with a hand-cranked machine. My parents would make a huge sign on butcher paper with tempera paint, announcing my celebration, and I got used to it, I guess. My mom would bake my cake and my dad would decorate it, always around a theme—it was anything from Holly Hobbie to a giant daisy cake, but it was always impressive. And still today, about a month before the big day rolls around, I start planning.

The details in question are few: Do I want a big party or just a dinner? Where should we have it? Who's bringing the rosé? But year to year, the menu is often quite repetitive. There are always steaks—fat, perfectly grilled rib eyes smeared with salty anchovy butter and drizzled with lemon juice—served with a great French red, like a Côtes du Rhône from Domaine Gramenon. And a handful of my favorite summery indulgences, like a buttery potato salad and Lay's potato chips.

My birthday bash is also a reliably good reflection of my culinary preferences; there are strong, salty flavors and gentle, herby ones, unabashedly American dishes and European standards. It's a menu that profiles who I am, in a way. And each year, I like to think it gets a little better.

SALTS AND SALTY THINGS

Salts

In my cooking, salt is pivotal. It has two major roles: first, as a flavor enhancer, brightening and intensifying flavors, and second, as a textural element. I choose which salt to use based on which of its roles is most important in the dish.

If I want to enhance background flavor, such as salting ingredients in the beginning of a cooking process or salting water for cooking, I use plain kosher salt. Kosher doesn't end up flavoring the final product, and it's cheaper, so it makes sense to use it where it's not as important—or for when you salt something using a large quantity of salt, like when preserving lemons.

If I only had one salt, I'd use *sel gris*, the chunky gray French sea salt. It has a clean, bright flavor, which makes it versatile, and a great texture that can be adjusted by grinding it to your preferred fineness. It's much cheaper than most finishing salts, which makes it a favorite for me at home.

I do also often use finishing salt, which is the champagne of salt. When salt is an important part of the final dish—when I want crunchy flakes that burst with flavor—I use a fine-flake sea salt. At our restaurants, we use Jacobsen Salt Co.'s snowy flakes because they're beautiful and relatively local. Cooking with finishing salt—using it in any way except sprinkled on top of food just before eating it—is a great way to waste money, so don't do it.

As a hard rule, I don't used iodized salt, which has a harsh, often metallic flavor that tastes synthetic to me. And although I like the taste of black pepper, I don't automatically pair salt and pepper together.

Salty Things

Salt isn't the only ingredient that can enhance a dish's flavor. From anchovies and capers to preserved lemons and olives, my kitchens host a wide array of salty things, which I use both as integral parts of dishes and as finishing touches.

Any good market should supply you with delicious versions of these ingredients. For more resources, see page 293.

Anchovies

Anchovies typically come one of two ways: whole and salt-packed, or filleted and packed in oil. I prefer salt-packed anchovies because they taste

continued

more like fish than like oil, and I feel more comfortable with the preserving process when salt is used. They must be rinsed before using, but they can be soaked or not, depending on how salty you want them to be. To soak them, first rinse the anchovies well. Place them in a large bowl and add water to cover, then let them soak for about 2 hours, changing the water every 30 minutes. Drain and rinse again, then set the anchovies aside to drip dry in a colander. When the fish have stopped dripping, they're ready to use.

I sneak finely chopped anchovies into braises and dressings—even meatloaf—because they offer an interesting depth of flavor you can't get from salt alone. To take the bones out of whole anchovies, use a small, sharp knife to remove one fillet at a time, slicing from the spine toward the belly on each side of the fish. (It's important to get the spine out, but it's okay to leave the littlest bones.)

Capers

Capers and caper berries are different parts of the same plant, the former being the unopened blossom of the plant's flower, the latter being its olive-shaped fruit. I use capers or caper berries where I want a briny, vegetal flavor. You can buy them packed in salt, which I prefer, or brined. Salt-packed capers should be soaked in multiple changes of water for an hour or two before using.

Olives

Olives taste like they look—dark, softer olives are riper, and thus have a gentler, sweeter, muskier flavor, while lighter-colored, firm green olives are sharper and more acidic, with a more vegetal flavor. My favorite olives are Niçoises. They're a middle-of-the-road olive, a bit acidic and a bit meaty, but not so sharp that they take over a dish. At The Whale Wins, we sell bowls of giant, fleshy *gordal* olives for snacking because they have a bright, citrusy flavor and a great meaty bite. And for looks, I'll go for almond-shaped, army-green picholine olives every time. If I'm not eating olives out of hand, I use them mostly pitted and chopped for vegetable salads, or for tapenade, one of my favorite things, which I love to smear on steak (see page 283 for the recipe).

Preserved Lemons

At my restaurants, we preserve our own lemons to use when we need a more floral salty flavor. It's a relatively simple process: We quarter them lengthwise almost all the way, pack them in kosher salt. Over the course of a few months, the salt turns into a silky brine. (See page 211 for the recipe.) For directions on how to use the peel, see Using Preserved Lemons, page 13.

radishes

green goddess dressing

PREP TIME: 25 MINUTES // TOTAL TIME: 25 MINUTES
MAKES: 2 GENEROUS CUPS DRESSING, ENOUGH TO SERVE 8

WHEN I LOOK FOR RADISHES, I want firm specimens about the size of a large marble, with bright, healthy greens. I personally have a thing for French Breakfast radishes—the oblong kind, which I split in half top to bottom if they're thicker than my thumb—but I also love Easter Egg radishes for their vibrant colors. I like to trim the greens to within about an inch of the radish's top, so guests can use the stem for dipping.

NOTE: If you have extra Green Goddess, you can thin it down and use it as a salad dressing the next day.

- 2 large bunches fresh radishes, trimmed and halved if large
- 1 cup mayonnaise, such as Best Foods
- 1 cup sour cream
- 2 whole anchovies, bones removed (see Salts and Salty Things: Anchovies, page 187), or 4 boneless fillets, chopped
- 1 garlic clove, minced
- 3 tablespoons extra-virgin olive oil

- 2 tablespoons freshly squeezed lemon juice (from about 1 medium lemon)
- 1 cup loosely packed fresh basil leaves
- ¼ cup loosely packed fresh tarragon leaves
- ¼ cup loosely packed fresh Italian parsley leaves
- ½ teaspoon kosher salt, plus more for seasoning

+ Arrange the radishes on a platter. In a heavy-duty blender or food processor, whirl the remaining ingredients until very smooth and a lovely pale-green color with tiny flecks of herbs. Taste and season with more salt, if necessary. Transfer half the dressing to a small bowl and serve with the radishes, replenishing the dressing as necessary.

marinated olives

thyme, garlic, lemon peel

PREP TIME: 10 MINUTES // TOTAL TIME: 15 MINUTES // MAKES 2 CUPS

IT'S EASY TO SAY THESE OLIVES are a great appetizer, but I actually make them totally selfishly, because they never get completely finished—which means that for the week or two after my birthday, there is always the perfect snack sitting in my refrigerator.

For information on where to purchase olives, see Resources, page 293.

NOTE: These taste best if allowed to marinate for at least a day (or, ideally, a full week) in the refrigerator.

---

1 tablespoon whole fennel seeds
2 cups extra-virgin olive oil
2 garlic cloves, thinly sliced
Julienned peel of 2 lemons
½ teaspoon red pepper flakes

3 sprigs fresh thyme
2 cups Niçoise, picholine, or
 Lucques olives, or a combination
 of your favorites

✦ Heat a small saucepan over medium heat. Add the fennel seeds and cook, shaking the pan occasionally, until the seeds are toasted and fragrant, 2 to 3 minutes. Turn the heat off. Add the oil, garlic, lemon peel, red pepper flakes, and thyme, and warm the oil slowly over low heat. After about 5 minutes, when the garlic just barely begins to sizzle, remove the pan from the heat.

✦ Put the olives in a quart-size container (such as a large glass jar), and pour the warm oil and seasonings over them. (It's easiest to scoop out the olives with a slotted spoon and add them first, then to pour the liquid over.) Allow the olives to cool to room temperature, then cover and refrigerate, at least overnight or up to 2 weeks, for the flavors to mingle. Let the olives to come to room temperature before serving.

grilled dry-aged rib-eye steaks

anchovy butter

PREP TIME: 10 MINUTES // TOTAL TIME: 45 MINUTES // SERVES 8

RIB EYE IS MY FAVORITE CUT of beef, and this, the method we use at Boat Street Café, is my favorite way to prepare it. Seared in a super-hot cast-iron pan or on the grill, cooked just to medium-rare, the meat gains a rich caramelization on both sides but still retains its softness. Spend time finding a perfect steak; you want dry-aged steak if you're ready to splurge on meat with rich, intense flavor. I tend to hover over my steaks to make sure they take on a deep brown crust, but they really don't require much attention once they're in the pan.

Even if you're squeamish about fat, you'll need to taste the triangular lip of fat on one end of the steak. I have a habit of treating mine like *lardo*, cutting it up into tiny pieces so I can get a bit of its rich, juicy flavor with each bite.

Because it's not always summer, I've written this recipe with instructions for cooking inside as well. If you don't have two cast-iron pans, do this in two batches. You won't need to add oil to the pan for the second batch.

4 (16-ounce) dry-aged bone-in
  rib-eye steaks, transferred to
  room temperature 30 minutes
  before cooking
6 tablespoons extra-virgin olive oil,
  divided (if cooking inside)

2 tablespoons crushed gray sea salt
  (see Resources, page 293)
2 lemons, halved
Anchovy Butter (recipe follows),
  softened

✦ If cooking outside: Preheat a charcoal grill for cooking over high heat, about 500 degrees F. Meanwhile, smear the steaks with 3 tablespoons of the olive oil, covering both sides of each steak, and season both sides of each with the salt. (You'll only use 3 tablespoons of the oil if cooking outside.)

✦ Brush the cooking grates clean. Grill the steaks for 5 to 8 minutes per side for 1½-inch-thick steaks, rotating the steaks 90 degrees halfway through cooking on each side, or until medium-rare inside. (Have tongs at the ready; cooking over a very hot grill means there may be flare-ups, in which case you'll need to move the steaks away from the flame immediately until the flame dies down. Smaller or boneless steaks will take about half the time.)

✦ If cooking inside: Preheat the oven to 450 degrees F. When the oven is hot, put two empty cast-iron pans into it and let them heat up for 15 minutes. Meanwhile, season the steaks per the instructions above.

continued

+ Place the hot pans on the stovetop over high heat. Immediately swirl half of the remaining 3 tablespoons oil into each pan. Add two of the steaks to each, and cook for 5 minutes undisturbed. When the meat is well caramelized on the first side, turn the steaks and cook for another 2 to 3 minutes for medium-rare. (Again, timing will depend on the size of the steaks; finish cooking thicker steaks in a 450-degree oven.) Add the lemons, cut side down, to the pan for the last minute or so.

+ Transfer the steaks to a platter and squeeze the juice of the lemons over the steaks. Let the steaks rest for 10 minutes before serving (you can grill the lemons if you like), half a steak per person, smeared with the anchovy butter.

anchovy butter

PREP TIME: 10 MINUTES // TOTAL TIME: 10 MINUTES // MAKES 1 CUP

OFTEN, WHEN I SMEAR A FLAVORFUL butter onto something, I want it to be spreadable, so I use it at room temperature, but the beauty of making this butter is that you can use some immediately and roll the rest into a log, which you can chill and slice for single servings later. (The butter is also great on grilled fish or roasted pork, or in place of regular butter when roasting vegetables.)

1 cup (2 sticks) unsalted butter, preferably European-style, softened	2 tablespoons finely chopped fresh thyme leaves
4 whole anchovies, bones removed (see Salts and Salty Things: Anchovies, page 187), or 8 boneless fillets, finely chopped	Grated zest of 1 medium lemon 2 tablespoons freshly squeezed lemon juice (from about 1 medium lemon) ½ teaspoon freshly ground black pepper

+ In the work bowl of a stand mixer fitted with the paddle attachment, whip the butter on high speed for 1 minute, until soft and fluffy. Add the anchovies, thyme, lemon zest and juice, and pepper, and mix on high for a minute more, stopping to scrape down the sides of the bowl once or twice.

+ To use at room temperature, transfer the butter to a bowl and serve. To store, dump the butter onto a sheet of waxed paper or plastic wrap, shape it into a log, and wrap it tightly. Refrigerate for at least 1 hour, or until the butter is firm, then wrap in plastic wrap and freeze up to 3 months. To serve, let the butter warm up enough to cut, and slice into, ½-inch-thick disks.

tomatoes

olive oil, vanilla bean salt

PREP TIME: 5 MINUTES // TOTAL TIME: 5 MINUTES // SERVES 8

ONCE, IN PARIS, I HAD A tomato salad with vanilla bean olive oil that changed my view of tomatoes forever. We tend to treat them as a strictly savory food, but combined with vanilla salt, they straddle the sweet-savory divide, giving up some of their sweetness with the heady aroma of vanilla but holding onto their acidity. Make this recipe only with summer's best acidic tomatoes, like beefsteak, green zebra, and Sungold cherry tomatoes.

If you're only using the vanilla bean salt for this recipe, quarter the salt recipe, making it with just ¼ cup salt and half of one vanilla bean.

8 large, ripe summer beefsteak
    tomatoes, sliced

About ¼ cup extra-virgin olive oil
Vanilla Bean Salt (page 288)

✦ Arrange the tomatoes on a large platter. Drizzle with the olive oil, then sprinkle with salt. Serve immediately.

JEFFRY MITCHELL (THE HUMAN), ARTIST AND ILLUSTRATOR

When I was in college at the University of Washington, Jeffry Mitchell was my printmaking teacher. Being in art school is fantastic, but being in art school with a professor who's generous, smart, and unpretentious made it outstanding. Jeffry was my mentor.

A year or two later, our roles reversed. I'd worked at the original Boat Street Café through college; Jeffry ended up there part-time, as a server. He was always traveling, teaching at colleges as a visiting professor and working as an artist in residence, but between adventures, he worked at the café. We became friends, then family.

One day, Jeffry gave me a giant stuffed hedgehog dog toy. I'd always *wanted* a dog, but at that point, I didn't *have* a dog. It was an odd gift, and it ended up forgotten under a chair. A few months later, I convinced my mom to buy a Lab for my dad, who quickly grew to love him, despite his best efforts to claim otherwise. I decided that I, too, needed one of those pups and claimed the last of the litter.

I named my dog Jule, a Swedish boy's name that I couldn't ever seem to remember. One night, Jule made a crashing, paw-pedaling dash for the hedgehog, which, at that point, was larger than he was. I knew then I needed to rename Jule for Jeffry, the human. Suddenly I had two best friends named Jeffry.

While Jeffry the dog has since passed, Jeffry the human is still very much part of my life. If you've eaten in my restaurants, you've seen his art; the caricatures on the walls of The Walrus and the Carpenter are his, as are the hand-drawn menus at our favorite seasonal feasts and the drawings that adorn this book's cover. Watching Jeffry make one of his signature "tablecloths" from butcher paper for our Lamb and Rosé Dinner (page 155) is like watching a talented kid make paper snowflakes, but his whimsical, heartfelt, sensual ceramics are found in galleries worldwide.

Jeffry is a source of constant inspiration for me—both artistically, still, and also personally. He's a dependable, tender, grown-up human version of that adorable puppy I still miss. And he always, *always* makes it to my birthday party.

potato salad

preserved lemon, chives

PREP TIME: 20 MINUTES // TOTAL TIME: 1 HOUR // SERVES 8

PEOPLE THINK OF POTATO SALAD AS a quintessentially American dish, but the way I make it, it doesn't quite fit into most football fans' culinary lexicon. It's also served warm; this is not the kind of potato salad that's going to go for a car ride before it gets served.

NOTE: If you'd like, use Brown Butter Vinaigrette (page 260) in place of the butter.

- 3 pounds golf ball–size yellow potatoes, whole, unpeeled
- 1 cup (2 sticks) unsalted butter, melted
- ½ cup thinly sliced preserved lemon peel, from about 1½ seeded preserved lemons (see Using Preserved Lemons, page 13)
- 1 tablespoon flaky sea salt, such as Maldon or Jacobsen (see Resources, page 293)
- ½ teaspoon freshly ground black pepper
- 2 tablespoons freshly squeezed lemon juice (from 1 medium lemon)
- ¾ cup minced chives or any combination of leafy green herbs such as parsley, tarragon, and dill

✦ Place the potatoes in a large pot and add cold water to cover by about 2 inches. Bring the water to a boil over high heat, then reduce the heat to medium and simmer the potatoes until tender when poked with a skewer, about 20 minutes for golf ball–size potatoes. Drain the potatoes in a colander and set them aside until they're cool enough to handle.

✦ In a large bowl, combine the butter, preserved lemon peel, salt, pepper, and lemon juice. When the potatoes are cool, cut them in half (or in quarters, for larger potatoes) and add them to the butter mixture. Stir to coat the potatoes with the butter, then fold in the chives. Serve warm or at room temperature.

peach cobbler

PREP TIME: 30 MINUTES // TOTAL TIME: 1 HOUR 40 MINUTES // SERVES 8

ORIGINAL BOAT STREET CAFÉ OWNER Susan Kaplan handed this recipe down to me when I took the reins, and although it's changed over the years, it's still a favorite. The method is a bit unusual: I dress unpeeled juicy peaches with lemon zest, then smear the batter on top, followed by a dousing of sugar and a bit of hot water. The result is a delicate crackly crust unrivaled in the world of cobblers. Use the same crust to top summer berries, if you prefer.

10 large peaches (about 4½ pounds), unpeeled, cut into 1-inch chunks
Zest and juice of 1 large lemon
½ cup (1 stick) unsalted butter, softened
2 cups sugar, divided

1½ cups (about 192 grams) all-purpose flour
2 teaspoons baking powder
1 teaspoon kosher salt
¾ cup whole milk
½ cup hot tap water
Heavy cream, for serving

+ Preheat the oven to 350 degrees F.

+ Put the peaches in a 9-by-13-inch (or similar) baking pan or gratin dish. Pat the peaches into a roughly even layer, then, using a zester or a Microplane, zest the lemon evenly over the fruit and squeeze the lemon juice evenly over the top.

+ In the work bowl of a stand mixer fitted with the paddle attachment, cream the butter and 1½ cups of the sugar on medium speed until sandy, about 1 minute. Add the flour, baking powder, and salt, and beat again for another 30 seconds, until all the flour is incorporated and the mixture is evenly crumbly. With the mixer on low speed, slowly add in the milk. Increase the speed to medium and beat until light and fluffy, about 2 minutes.

+ Plop the batter in 6 large blobs over the top of the peaches. With an offset spatula or small knife, carefully spread the batter evenly over the fruit, so it's no more than about ½ inch thick in any one place.

+ Sprinkle the remaining ½ cup sugar directly over the batter. Drizzle the hot water evenly over the sugar, using it to melt the sugar into the topping. (Use it all. It's a strange method, but it works.)

+ Bake the cobbler for 70 to 80 minutes, or until the top is browned and cracked. (A toothpick inserted into the topping should come out dry—be sure to check in a few places.)

+ Let the cobbler sit for about a half an hour to firm up before serving warm in big bowls, with heavy cream poured on top.

FALL

Early Fall Put-Up Party

Preserved Lemons *211*
Fresh Bay Leaves

Pickled Turnips *212*
Toasted Curry, Garlic

Pickled Fennel *213*
Arból Chilis, Orange Peel

Pickled Fresh Plum Jam *214*
Chilis, Bay, Coriander

Pickled Carrots *217*
Saffron, Star Anise

Pickled Chanterelles *218*
Thyme, Garlic, Olive Oil

Simplest Pickled Shallots *222*

Pickled Beets *223*
Mustard Seeds, Tellicherry Peppercorns

Pickled Watermelon *224*
Lemon Peel, Bay

We had a pickle plate at Boat Street Café about fifteen years ago. In the beginning, I remember people making fun of me, because at the time, the pickling phenomenon hadn't yet started. It seemed a bit odd, but I felt pickles were necessities. When I traveled in Europe, I learned how a dish can be more well rounded when it has an acidic food as a component, and I didn't want to leave my newfound pickle-eating habit behind. So I brought home the pickles I loved most. I love making them because they're a quick way to give foods a huge burst of flavor, and because with so many possible pickling ingredients, there are infinite flavor combinations.

At Boat Street, I first started serving our pickled prunes with Boat Street Chicken Liver Pâté (page 74). People asked to take them home frequently enough that, with the encouragement of my mom, Shirlee, I started Boat Street Pickles, a company that now produces jarred pickled fruit. We pickled on Sundays and Mondays initially, in Boat Street's kitchen when the restaurant was closed, and slowly ramped up our little operation until it became what it is today—and those pretty jars are available all over the world.

Now, of course, pickles are as ubiquitous on restaurant plates as they are in basements nationwide. In my restaurants, we rarely process our pickles to be shelf stable—not because we don't like to, but because we simply don't have the space to store them in anything but small quantities. I also prefer refrigerator pickles because it typically means using the fruits and vegetables a month or two after they've passed their season, when I pine for them most.

The recipes that follow are all for refrigerator pickles, also known as quick pickles. Gather a few friends and make as many of the recipes as you'd like. You can process them to be shelf stable, if you prefer, using the directions provided by your canning jar's manufacturer. I always use wide-mouth jars for canning because they seem easiest.

preserved lemons
fresh bay leaves

PREP TIME: 15 MINUTES // TOTAL TIME: 1 MONTH // MAKES 6
SPECIAL EQUIPMENT: ONE 1½-QUART-SIZE JAR WITH A LID

THESE DAYS, IT'S POSSIBLE TO BUY good preserved lemons in jars, but it's also possible to buy terrible, metallic-tasting ones, so at the restaurants, we often make our own. Luckily, it's a pretty simple project.

NOTE: After the initial process, you'll have to add additional salt to the jar for the first few days, as the salt dissolves into a brine.

---

12 medium organic lemons
1 (3-pound) box coarse kosher salt
(see Resources, page 293)

4 fresh bay leaves

✦ Wash the lemons well and set 6 of them aside for juicing. Using a small, sharp knife, cut the dry stems off the remaining 6 lemons—just enough so you see their flesh poking through. Starting with the cut side, quarter the lemons the long way, slicing only about ⅞ of the way through, so each lemon is held intact by its blossom (pointy) end.

✦ Next, pour a roughly ½-inch layer of salt into the bottom of a 1½-quart jar. Fill a medium bowl with about 2 cups of the salt. Using your hands, roll the lemons in the salt one at a time, using your fingers to pack it onto the cut sides of each lemon. Add 3 lemons to the jar, add salt to cover, and stuff 2 bay leaves down into the jar. Add the remaining lemons, salt, and bay leaves, then juice the remaining 6 lemons into the jar, seeds and all. Twist and turn and shake the jar to encourage the salt to settle, add salt to cover the lemons, and close the jar.

✦ Let the lemons sit on the counter at room temperature for about 4 hours. As the lemons begin to lose their juices, the salt will dissolve and settle. Top the lemons off with more salt, then repeat again in the morning. (Note that you *must* keep the lemons covered with about ½ inch of salt or salty liquid, or the air will reach the lemons and they will rot.) Store the lemons at room temperature in sight for a week or so, gently shaking and turning the jar and adding salt every day or two as needed, until the salt has all dissolved and the lemons are stored in a milky liquid. Transfer the jar to a cold, dark room and store for at least 1 month (or up to 4 months) before using, or transfer to the refrigerator and store for up to 1 year.

pickled turnips

toasted curry, garlic

PREP TIME: 20 MINUTES // TOTAL TIME: 1 HOUR 20 MINUTES // MAKES 1 QUART
SPECIAL EQUIPMENT: 1 QUART-SIZE OR 2 PINT-SIZE JARS WITH LIDS

I LIKE USING BABY TURNIPS BECAUSE they're the sweetest, and because at the restaurant, they're pretty when we serve them as a condiment for pâtés and terrines. At home, I mostly eat them straight out of the jar.

NOTE: If you can't find the toasted curry blend, substitute a mixture of toasted coriander and cumin seeds.

4 bunches baby (golf ball–size)
    turnips (about 1½ pounds total),
    leaves trimmed to ½ inch from
    top, root ends trimmed, and
    halved
2 cups white wine vinegar
1 cup water

⅓ cup sugar
1 tablespoon toasted Sri Lankan
    curry blend (see Inside the Jar,
    page 225)
1 teaspoon kosher salt
3 cloves garlic, very thinly sliced
1 fresh bay leaf

✦ In a large saucepan, combine all the ingredients. Bring the mixture to a boil, reduce the heat to a simmer, and cook, uncovered, for 6 to 8 minutes, or until you can bite through the turnips but they still have some crunch. Remove the pan from the heat and let the turnips sit until they reach room temperature. Transfer the turnips to jars, pour the brine on top, and store in the refrigerator for up to 1 month.

pickled fennel

arból chilis, orange peel

PREP TIME: 15 MINUTES // TOTAL TIME: 1 HOUR 15 MINUTES // MAKES 3 PINTS
SPECIAL EQUIPMENT: 3 PINT-SIZE JARS WITH LIDS

OUT OF THE JAR, THIS VERSION of pickled fennel tastes as much of orange and spice as it does of fennel, which makes it the perfect punchy topping for the Ricotta Tartine with Pickled Scapes and Fennel (page 160). I also love it smeared on smoked-fish toast; try topping Grilled Bread (page 277) with Herring Butter (page 68) and layering the fennel on top.

NOTE: For this recipe, you'll need about 2 pounds of fennel if the bulbs are trimmed, or 2½ pounds if the fronds are still attached.

---

2 medium fennel bulbs, white
    and very light-green parts only,
    cored and sliced ⅛ inch thick
2½ cups champagne vinegar (see
    Resources, page 293) or white
    wine vinegar
1 cup water

1 cup sugar
3 dried arból or japones chilis
2 fresh bay leaves
Julienned peel of 1 medium orange
1 tablespoon fennel seeds
1 teaspoon Tellicherry peppercorns
1 teaspoon kosher salt

✦ In a large saucepan, combine all the ingredients. Bring the mixture to a boil, reduce the heat to a simmer, and cook for 5 minutes, uncovered, or until you can bite through the fennel but it still has some crunch. (The fennel will give up some liquid as it cooks, so stir and pat it down occasionally to encourage it to sink down into the pan.) Remove the pan from the heat and let the fennel sit until it reaches room temperature. Transfer the fennel to jars, pour the brine on top, and store in the refrigerator for up to 1 month.

pickled fresh plum jam
chilis, bay, coriander

PREP TIME: 20 MINUTES // TOTAL TIME: 2 HOURS 30 MINUTES // MAKES 4 PINTS
SPECIAL EQUIPMENT: 4 PINT-SIZE JARS WITH LIDS

IN FRANCE, PÂTÉ IS OFTEN SERVED with condiments that defy the American definition of a pickle. They're often sweet and savory at the same time, served in little piles next to toasts and perhaps a dab of mustard.

I had pickled plums for the first time in Provence with my mother, when we went to take cooking classes there from Patricia Wells. It was the first time I closed Boat Street Café for a vacation after I bought it, and when I returned, they were the first things I added to the menu—which later led to the pickled prunes that inspired the launch of Boat Street Pickles. Try it served over grilled pork chops or duck.

3 dried arból or japones chilis
5 pounds fresh, ripe plums, pitted
   and cut into quarters or eighths
4 cups sugar
2 cups cider vinegar or white wine
   vinegar

3 fresh bay leaves
Julienned peel of 1 large orange
1 teaspoon whole coriander seeds
1 teaspoon kosher salt

✦ First, place a few small plates in the freezer. You'll use these to test the jam for doneness.

✦ Break the chilis open and dump out about half the seeds. Crush the rest of the chilis in your hands, then put them into a heavy pot large enough to hold all the plums with at least 2 inches of room at the top. Add the plums, sugar, vinegar, bay leaves, orange peel, coriander seeds, and salt. Cook over low heat, stirring occasionally, until the sugar dissolves, about 5 minutes, then bring the mixture to a gentle boil and cook, skimming off the peach-colored foam that forms on the top of the jam with a spoon, for 45 to 60 minutes. Since both stoves and plum juiciness differ, it's important to test the jam for doneness; you'll know it's ready when a teaspoon of it gels on a frozen plate in a minute or two, so go by the texture of the jam more than by time. (Note that you will still see the plums' skin when the jam is done.)

✦ Transfer the jam to jars, let cool to room temperature, and refrigerate. The jam will keep up to 3 months unopened, then for about 2 weeks once opened.

pickled carrots

saffron, star anise

PREP TIME: 15 MINUTES // TOTAL TIME: 1 HOUR 15 MINUTES // MAKES 1 QUART
SPECIAL EQUIPMENT: 1 QUART-SIZE OR 2 PINT-SIZE JARS WITH LIDS

STUDDED WITH STAR ANISE AND PAINTED golden with dainty threads of saffron, these carrots win the beauty pageant every time. Use as much saffron as fits your taste and budget; it doesn't take much to give the brine a pretty color, but it takes two healthy pinches to infuse the carrots with saffron's lovely honey flavor.

As long as the stems are clean and sturdy, I leave about one inch of stem attached to the top of each carrot.

2 bunches (1½ pounds) medium
    carrots, peeled (about 15
    carrots)
3 cups cider vinegar
1½ cups water
½ cup sugar
3 whole star anise

Heaping ½ teaspoon saffron
    threads (2 pinches)
Julienned peel of half a medium
    lemon
1 tablespoon yellow mustard seeds
1 teaspoon kosher salt

✦ If necessary, trim the carrots to fit the jar(s) you're using; halve any carrots fatter than a man's thumb lengthwise. In a large saucepan, combine all the ingredients. Bring the mixture to a boil, reduce the heat to a simmer, and cook for 12 to 14 minutes, uncovered, or until you can bite through the carrots but they still have some crunch. Remove the pan from the heat and let the carrots sit until they reach room temperature. Transfer the carrots to jars, pour the brine on top, and store in the refrigerator for up to 1 month.

pickled chanterelles

thyme, garlic, olive oil

PREP TIME: 25 MINUTES // TOTAL TIME: 30 MINUTES, PLUS OVERNIGHT BRINING TIME
MAKES 3 PINTS // SPECIAL EQUIPMENT: 3 PINT-SIZE JARS WITH LIDS

CHANTERELLES AND PORCINI ARE MY TWO favorite mushrooms. Conveniently, chanterelles are much cheaper—and so prolific in the Pacific Northwest that if you go mushrooming in the fall, you can often come home with paper grocery bags full of them. Pickled when they're tiny and stored in oil, they become a great condiment for everything from Roasted Chicken (page 257) to simple grilled salmon. You can also use them in place of the pickled fennel and scapes in the Ricotta Tartine with Pickled Scapes and Fennel (page 160).

Trim off the dried ends of any chanterelles that seem to need it. Halve or quarter the mushrooms if large. If they're tiny (marble-size caps or smaller), just leave them whole—what's important is that they're all roughly the same size.

1½ pounds small chanterelle
    mushrooms, well cleaned (see
    Cleaning Mushrooms, page 11)
3 cups white wine vinegar
1½ cups water
3 big sprigs fresh thyme
4 cloves garlic, thinly sliced

2 dried arból or japones chilis
Julienned peel of half a lemon
2 teaspoons kosher salt
1 teaspoon Tellicherry peppercorns
1 fresh bay leaf
About 3½ cups extra-virgin
    olive oil

✦ Put the mushrooms in a large bowl. In a large saucepan, combine the vinegar, water, thyme, garlic, chilis, lemon peel, salt, peppercorns, and bay leaf. Bring the mixture to a boil, stir until the salt has dissolved, then pour the mixture over the mushrooms. Cut a piece of parchment paper to fit the bowl and place it on top of the liquid, then use a plate (or something else that fits just inside the rim of the bowl) to weight the mushrooms down. Let the mixture cool to room temperature, then refrigerate overnight.

✦ Drain the mushrooms, pick out and discard the aromatics, and transfer the mushrooms to 3 pint jars. Add olive oil to each jar until the chanterelles are completely covered. Seal and refrigerate for at least a day (or up to 6 months) before serving.

SHIRLEE ERICKSON,
BOAT STREET PICKLES

When I was growing up, there was a closet under the stairs in the basement of our house in Woodinville, WA. It was there that my mom, Shirlee Erickson, stacked the edible memories of our garden each year, jar after jar of green beans and peaches and strawberry jam. Rumor has it that as a little girl, I preferred snacking in the strawberry patch to actually picking them for the jam, but as I got older, I became more helpful. Ultimately, she's the one I credit with my passion for putting things in jars.

The thing is, canning encapsulates my mom's talents. She's organized, sweet, and stable, and spicy only when necessary. My mom has always been the one to keep things tidy and flowing smoothly in my life. When I decided to buy the original Boat Street Café, I'd just returned from Europe, and I didn't even have a liquid bank account. It was my mom who—with the full support of my dad and the rest of my family—gave me the organizational power to get it all done. Having just retired, she volunteered to do everything from baking to bookkeeping, her roles changing to fit whatever assistance I needed most, as they still do today. She's always insisted she thinks helping me is more fun than being retired, anyway, and I've never liked the financial aspect of running a business.

To be honest, in the pickle department, things haven't changed much today. At Boat Street Pickles, although I'm the so-called creative force, it's Shirlee—known by her first name to all my employees—who manages the show, as she has from the start, overseeing the business from orchard to jar. At home, she walks around my kitchen with more authority than I feel I have sometimes, cleaning and arranging and helping in just the right way. She has every right to retire for real eventually, and I hope she will. In theory, at least. I know that no matter what her official title is—bookkeeper, manager, supermom, or blackberry pie maker extraordinaire—she'll always be there, like those jars under the stairs.

simplest pickled shallots

PREP TIME: 20 MINUTES // TOTAL TIME: 20 MINUTES,
PLUS ABOUT 2 HOURS BRINING TIME // MAKES 3 PINTS
SPECIAL EQUIPMENT: 3 PINT-SIZE JARS WITH LIDS

THE SIMPLEST FORM OF PICKLING IS, of course, blending something with vinegar and just a touch of sugar and salt. It's how I like to pickle shallots, both because it gives them a pure, bright flavor and because it's almost painfully easy. I serve them with everything from Boat Street Chicken Liver Pâté (page 74) to Roasted Chicken (page 257).

I prefer to shave shallots on a mandoline because it makes them evenly thin, but you can cut them to ⅛ inch thick with a sharp knife if you prefer.

2 pounds shallots, shaved into
⅛-inch-thick rounds
4 cups champagne vinegar (see
Resources, page 293)

1½ teaspoons sugar
1½ teaspoons kosher salt

✦ In a mixing bowl, stir together all the ingredients. Let the mixture sit at room temperature for about 2 hours, stirring occasionally, until the shallots have softened enough to sink into the vinegar.

✦ Transfer the shallots to 3 pint jars, add the vinegar mixture to cover, and seal. Refrigerate until ready to use, up to 2 months.

pickled beets

mustard seeds, tellicherry peppercorns

PREP TIME: 15 MINUTES // TOTAL TIME: 2 HOURS // MAKES 1 QUART
SPECIAL EQUIPMENT: 1 QUART-SIZE OR 2 PINT-SIZE JARS WITH LIDS

IF I COULD CREATE AN ULTIMATE appetizer plate, it would have cheese and nuts and olives and charcuterie, and a great combination of pickles, including these earthy pickled beets. You can use large beets, as directed here, or beets of any size—adjust the cooking time accordingly, so they come off the heat when they're cooked but still a bit crunchy.

If you'd like to save the beet greens, you can use them in place of the nettles in the Lentil Salad (page 94).

2 bunches (1¾ pounds) baseball-size beets (about 6 beets), trimmed, peeled, and quartered	2 tablespoons mustard seeds
	1 tablespoon Tellicherry peppercorns
3 cups cider vinegar	1 tablespoon coriander seeds
1 cup water	1 fresh bay leaf
½ cup sugar	1 teaspoon kosher salt

➤ In a large saucepan, combine all the ingredients. Bring the mixture to a boil, then reduce the heat to a simmer, and cook, uncovered, for 20 to 25 minutes, depending on the size and age of the beets, or until you can bite through the beets but they still have some crunch. Remove the pan from the heat and let the beets sit until they reach room temperature. Transfer the beets to jars, pour the brine on top, and store in the refrigerator for up to 1 month.

pickled watermelon
lemon peel, bay

PREP TIME: 15 MINUTES // TOTAL TIME: 2 HOURS // MAKES 3 PINTS
SPECIAL EQUIPMENT: 3 PINT-SIZE JARS WITH LIDS

IT WAS A MISTAKE, REALLY. WATERMELON is actually one of my least favorite melons, because to me, the texture of raw watermelon flesh isn't as luscious as, say, a good cantaloupe. I was going through an old American pickling book, pickling just about anything I could get my hands on. I wondered why no one talked about pickled watermelon meat and what a quick bath in vinegar might do to that gritty flesh.

In this case, pickling changes everything. The texture of the flesh turns into something of a jelly, almost like a French *pâte de fruit*. I love mixing the chopped pickle (rind and all) with preserved lemon, olive oil, and mint, and serving it over grilled lamb tongue.

NOTE: Be sure to wash the outside of the watermelon well before beginning.

Half a 5-pound watermelon
3 cups white wine vinegar
¾ cup water
¾ cup sugar
2 teaspoons Tellicherry
   peppercorns

Julienned peel of half a medium
   lemon
1 fresh bay leaf
½ teaspoon kosher salt

✦ Cut the watermelon into 3 long wedges, then cut each wedge lengthwise into ½-inch-thick triangles. Layer the triangles in a deep, wide pot.

✦ In a large saucepan, combine the vinegar, water, sugar, peppercorns, lemon peel, bay leaf, and salt. Bring the mixture to a boil, reduce to a simmer, and cook for a minute or two, until the sugar has dissolved completely.

✦ Pour the liquid mixture over the watermelon, bring to a gentle boil, and cook, dunking the top watermelon wedges under the liquid occasionally, for about 45 minutes, or until the white part of the watermelon is transparent, the red part looks jelly-like, and the green rind is soft enough to bite through. (If the watermelon wedges bob up to the top of the liquid, you may need to cut a piece of parchment paper to fit the pan, place it on top of the liquid, and weight the paper with a small plate.)

✦ Remove the pan from the heat and let the watermelon sit until it reaches room temperature. Carefully transfer the watermelon to jars, pour the brine on top, and store in the refrigerator for up to 1 week.

INSIDE THE JAR

Pickles are only as good as the ingredients that go into the jar. Of course it's important to think about what flavors you want your pickles to have, besides whatever it is you're pickling. But it's equally important to buy your ingredients intelligently, purchasing only a little bit at a time, from a store where the turnover is high, so that the herbs and spices you use have a chance to shine. In Seattle, we're lucky to have World Spice Merchants (see Resources, page 293), a Pike Place Market shop with a dizzying array of fresh spices and herbs. World Spice ships almost anywhere, but most large natural grocery stores have bulk spices with good turnover. The herbs, spices, and aromatics below are my pickling staples.

Chilis

Dried chilis are an addiction for me. Most often, I use arból or japones chilis, which, when dried, gain a floral characteristic that's difficult to replicate without actually using flowers. They do a great job of adding heat and depth to whatever you're pickling, but since you don't eat the chilis themselves, they don't actually make your food spicy.

Fresh Bay Leaves

Bay is my favorite aromatic herb. It grows so well in Seattle, and I'm constantly bombarded by its heady fragrance in my backyard. I don't like dry bay because the flavor isn't as bright, and because it sometimes breaks into shards if you end up with a leaf in your mouth, which is never pleasant. If you want to plant one new herb in your garden, try bay.

Fresh Citrus Peel

I consistently use citrus peel (along with bay) more than any other addition to my pickles. I like that, in many ways, it's more aromatic than flavorful, which means that it contributes to the overall experience rather than overwhelming the flavor of whatever you're pickling.

Garlic

It's a classic pickle ingredient for a reason; sliced into a brine, garlic adds flavor and heat. Note that garlic will get hotter and hotter as it sits in pickle brine, so use it sparingly.

continued

Saffron

In addition to lending a gorgeous golden hue, saffron, the dried threads of crocus flowers, has a delicate flavor that reminds me of citrus, honey, and hay. I add it to pickles when I'm making something that already has a soft flavor—cauliflower, carrots, or turnips, for example. Note that the richness of a pickle's saffron flavor grows as the pickles sit.

Sri Lankan Curry

In Seattle, World Spice Merchants makes a Sri Lankan–style curry blend we use in the pickled apricots for Boat Street Pickles, but it's great in just about everything, from cauliflower to celery root to Pickled Turnips (page 212). It has a blend of coriander, cumin, fennel, fenugreek, cassia, clove, cardamom, chilis, and black pepper that I've never dared to try to replicate.

Star Anise

Star anise comes from the fruit of a Southeast Asian evergreen tree, and though it's not related to the anise plant, it has the same warm, astringent flavor. When I cook with it, it always reminds me of gently spiced winter foods—North African or Indian stews, for example. I often use star anise in pickles in place of clove, when I want a warm spice. Note that, like clove, it's strong enough to overtake almost any other flavor, so use it sparingly.

Tellicherry Peppercorns

Tellicherry peppercorns, grown on India's Malabar Coast, are the pungent variety that gave the British East India Company strength as a spice-trading merchant. Think of using the more expensive, more flavorful Tellicherry peppercorns as the pepper equivalent of choosing a great heirloom tomato varietal in midsummer instead of buying grape tomatoes at a grocery store in January. They're left to ripen longer on the vine, rather than picked unripe, which gives anything you add them to a more exotic, complex flavor.

Yellow Mustard Seeds

It may seem the most obvious spice to use when pickling, but it should be; mustard seeds add a soft spiciness that rounds out almost any flavor, and inside a jar, they always look dainty and attractive.

Normandy Dinner

Local Oysters *233*
Champagne Vinegar Mignonette

Parsnip Soup *237*
Leeks, Apples, Walnut Oil

Mussels in Cider *238*
Dijon, Crème Fraîche, Tarragon

Celery, Kohlrabi, Apple, and Walnut Salad *240*
Walnut Oil Vinaigrette

Braised Pork Shoulder *243*
Served Crispy with Pork Demi

Braised Cabbage *245*
Apples, Caraway, Cream

French Apple Cake *247*

SERVES *8*

THERE IS A DEPENDABLE TIDAL RHYTHM to life on the coast of Normandy. It's a slow, methodical sort of place, where even the shortest meals pay homage to history and tradition. At our annual Normandy Dinner at Boat Street Café, we follow the same ebb and tide of the classic French meal, starting with cider and muscadet under the twinkling lights on the patio. If you come early, you'll hear my father marvel the same way he does every year at how much he enjoys a good oyster. "I never ate a lot of oysters until Renee contaminated me," he'll say. And just as your fingertips turn to ice in the November rain, one of the servers, perhaps Shannon or Phyllis, will appear with a cup of warm soup, and you'll wrap your hands around it and wonder what wave comes next.

Like any big dinner we do, the advance orchestration is a huge part of our success. We braise the pork (usually about fifty pounds of it) the evening before the meal. We plan the pacing of the courses carefully. We order my favorite Normand cider, Eric Bordelet's "Sidre." Ultimately, we want to ensure that behind Boat Street's foggy windows, guests are transported by the flavors of Normandy—apples, cider, shellfish, butter, cream, and intensely flavorful meat—the same way I am each time I visit France's northwest corner. I know I'm successful when, as we linger over tiny glasses of calvados and perhaps the last bit of creamy Washington cheese (our favorite is a Camembert-style round from Kurtwood Farms called Dinah's Cheese), I hear someone mention plane tickets.

SHUCKING OYSTERS

The next time you visit The Walrus and the Carpenter, watch the shuckers. When they open a Northwest oyster, they start at the hinge end, prying the oyster open with what looks like almost zero effort. Then they cut the oyster's muscle from its shell, turning the flesh over and revealing the oyster's smooth, plump side.

In France, it's usually done differently: instead of the hinge end, they shuck the oyster from the side, where the muscle attaches. Then they release the fleshy part of the muscle from the oyster's top shell, leaving the firm part of the muscle attached to the bottom shell to prove the creature is still alive. I love that tradition because it means that after you eat the muscle, you can use the flat side of a fork to scrape the scallop-like attachment from the shell, then drink the oyster's liquor separately. Although I hew to American convention at my restaurants (including serving oysters ice-cold, per health department standards, instead of just cool, as in France), I like how visceral and drawn out the experience is in France.

Of course, I do have my favorite oysters. In the Pacific Northwest, I love Hama Hamas, Blue Pools, Emerald Acres Treasure Coves, Taylor Shellfish Totten Virginicas, and Hog Island Sweetwaters.

To open an oyster using the typical American technique, the hinge method, you'll need well-rinsed oysters, an oyster knife, a towel, and a pair of heavy-duty gloves.

If you've never opened an oyster before, start with a soft, clean towel in your left hand. Hold the cupped part of the oyster in the palm of your hand on top of the towel, with the hinge (pointed) end toward your wrist. (You can put a heavy-duty glove on the hand holding the oyster, if you're shucking a lot of oysters or feel accident-prone). Using your right hand, insert the point of the knife into the hinge of the oyster, pressing gently on the hinge until you feel it pop open. (Some people say you press the oyster onto the knife instead of the knife into the oyster; in either case, placement is more important than pressure. This process should not cause you to break a sweat.) Wipe the knife clean on the towel. With the oyster just partway open, slip the knife's blade into the shell. Carefully follow the right side of the top shell with the knife to cut the oyster muscle free, then remove the top shell. Wipe the knife again, then carefully cut the muscle off the bottom shell, taking care to reserve as much of the oyster's natural liquor as possible. (If you prefer, use the knife to turn the oyster over in the bottom shell.) Remove any sneaky shell pieces that may be wandering around in the liquor, and serve immediately. (If you're left-handed, you'll need to start with the oyster in your right hand, turn the oyster over, and adjust these directions accordingly.)

local oysters

champagne vinegar mignonette

PREP TIME: 10 MINUTES, PLUS SHUCKING TIME // TOTAL TIME: 10 MINUTES,
PLUS SHUCKING TIME // SERVES 8

ALTHOUGH I PERSONALLY PREFER EATING OYSTERS plain or with a squeeze of lemon, it's impossible to ignore the allure of a perfect mignonette. I serve it, made with a simple mixture of shallots and good champagne vinegar, and a grinding of black pepper, in a shallow bowl before dinner, so guests can add as much as they'd like to each oyster.

NOTE: Store fresh oysters in the refrigerator, cupped side down, on a plate covered with a damp towel.

---

1 large shallot, minced
1 cup champagne vinegar (see
    Resources, page 293)
2 dozen fresh local oysters, chilled

Freshly ground black pepper
    (optional)
1 medium lemon, cut into wedges

✦ In a serving bowl, stir together the shallots and vinegar. Refrigerate until ready to serve, up to 2 days.

✦ Shuck the oysters immediately before serving (see Shucking Oysters, page 232), and serve the mignonette, dusted with pepper to taste, in a small bowl alongside the oysters, along with a bowl of the lemon wedges.

L'ÉCAILLER NORMAND
HUITRES
RMANDIE
"La B
iron"
www.hui
mandie.fr
15,30€

STÉPHANE LE BOZEC, OYSTER SELLER

Weekends on *rue Cler* in Paris's seventh arrondissement, Stéphane Le Bozec rolls a red-roofed cart onto the patio at Brasserie Aux PTT, shucking ten or twelve types of briny French oysters for folks who enjoy them *sur place* with a glass of white wine. Stéphane gets his oysters from a man named Patrick Liron, a jovial oyster broker based in Blainville-sur-Mer, on Normandy's windy Cotentin Peninsula. Since the 1970s, oysters have been raised there, in mesh bags strapped to low tables that peek out of the water as Europe's most extreme tide rushes out the long, flat beach twice each day.

But Normandy is different. In most oyster-growing regions, including those in France and most of the Pacific Northwest, the nutrients in river water help define an oyster's taste. Some beaches in Normandy are unique in that there are no river outlets, which means the oysters there are exceptionally briny because they never get flushed with freshwater. And unlike typical American oyster growers, who depend on boats to transport oysters at high tide, the Normand *ostréiculteurs* use giant tractors hooked up to flatbed trailers to get their work done in the time surrounding low tide—that, and good old-fashioned manpower.

Stéphane says oysters are like children; you have to take care of them and respect their intrinsic differences. His oysters are coddled. They're shaken in just the right way on a regular basis, and sorted, forever sorted, so they can be moved into bags with equal-sized neighbors as they grow. In Cotentin, an oyster from one town can taste completely different from that of the next town, simply because the land protects the water from the western winds more or less. And when Stéphane sells his shellfish in Paris, on a street that seems to have made him its volunteer mayor, he can tell you about them all—about how those winds can change their brininess from week to week, and about how their flavors change with the seasons. He loves it when customers ask how a particular oyster is tasting that particular week.

I met him in 2010, when I was researching oysters in preparation for opening The Walrus and the Carpenter. At the restaurant, our local oysters aren't as briny, and they're generally a bit fatter, with less liquor. But with each bivalve that leaves our bar, I hope we deliver the same message that Stéphane does: it's not the staff at Walrus who grow the oysters. It's the sea and its *meroir*, the gift of time, and the hard, cold, salty everyday work of oyster farmers that make it happen. We just have to open them.

parsnip soup

leeks, apples, walnut oil

PREP TIME: 30 MINUTES // TOTAL TIME: 1 HOUR // SERVES 8, WITH LEFTOVERS

THERE'S A NASTY RUMOR THAT SEATTLE can be unlovely on a drizzly fall evening, when the temperature hovers just above freezing. But at our annual Normandy Dinner at Boat Street Café, held each November, I wouldn't have it any other way. Guests gather outdoors under twinkling lights, sipping French cider (see Resources, page 293) and slurping local oysters. Just when the cold sets in, before we head inside for dinner, I serve soup, typically in paper cups, so people can warm their hands.

This version is a cousin of potato leek soup, with the voluptuous texture of that old French classic but a flavor that relies mostly on sweet fall parsnips. This recipe serves six on its own as a hearty dinner, eight to twelve as a small first course, or up to twenty in small tasting cups. You can halve the recipe, but I find it's one of the best things to have in the refrigerator for a quick lunch.

6 tablespoons (¾ stick) unsalted butter

3 large leeks, white and light-green parts only, washed well, halved lengthwise, and cut into ½-inch-thick slices (about 4½ cups total)

3 medium sweet-tart apples, such as Honeycrisp, peeled, cored, and cut into 1-inch pieces

2 pounds parsnips, peeled and cut into 1-inch pieces

2 fist-size white potatoes (about 1 pound), peeled and cut into 1-inch pieces

2 quarts chicken broth

1 cup heavy cream

1 tablespoon flaky sea salt, such as Maldon or Jacobsen (see Resources, page 293)

Toasted walnut oil, for drizzling (see Resources, page 293)

✦ Heat a large soup pot over medium heat. Add the butter. When the butter has melted, add the leeks and cook, stirring occasionally, until they begin to soften, about 5 minutes. Add the apples, parsnips, potatoes, and chicken broth, and bring the mixture to a boil. Reduce to a simmer and cook, covered, for 25 to 30 minutes, or until the vegetables are totally tender, stirring once or twice during cooking. In a heavy-duty blender or food processor, carefully puree the soup in batches until completely smooth. Return the soup to the pot and bring to a low simmer. Gently stir in the cream and the salt, adding more to taste, stirring until the salt dissolves completely before adding more. Serve the soup hot, with a drizzle of walnut oil on top, about 1 teaspoon per bowl.

mussels in cider

dijon, crème fraîche, tarragon

PREP TIME: 30 MINUTES // TOTAL TIME: 30 MINUTES // SERVES 8

IN BLAINVILLE-SUR-MER, A TINY TOWN ON Normandy's Cotentin Peninsula, there's a quirky little restaurant called La Cale, whose official street address is "La Plage," or, simply, "the beach." It overlooks the tidal flats that stretch five kilometers into the sea—an area that accounts for more than 10 percent of France's oyster production—but at high tide, when all traces of aquaculture disappear, it's simply a beachfront bistro with a few legs of lamb on an open hearth. It's homey, complete with picnic tables and a "serve yourself " rule that explains why patrons cut their own bread, fetch their own water, and choose their own wine from a shelf next to the bar. The rule does not explain why the room is adorned in giant needlepoints of various nudes, both male and female, but the artworks add a je ne sais quoi that I'd miss if I returned to find them replaced with something more modest.

When you order mussels there, they come in the pot they were cooked in, steamed in cider and topped with a generous dollop of crème fraîche, which whoever has thought to grab a ladle gets to stir into them just before serving. This recipe is similar. And as you do at La Cale, you should eat a small mussel first, then use its shell as a utensil to pry the mussels out of the remaining shells.

3 tablespoons unsalted butter	Freshly squeezed lemon juice, for
2 large shallots, thinly sliced (about	seasoning
1 cup)	Kosher salt
2 tablespoons Dijon mustard	¾ cup crème fraîche
3 cups dry hard cider	½ cup loosely packed whole tarra-
3 pounds mussels, cleaned and	gon leaves (no stems)
debearded	Crusty bread, for serving

✦ In a large, high-sided saucepan or soup pot, melt the butter over medium-low heat. When the butter has melted, add the shallots and cook, stirring, until the shallots are soft, about 5 minutes. Whisk in the mustard, add the cider, then increase the heat to medium-high. Add the mussels and cook, covered, until they begin to open, about 5 minutes. Remove the lid and begin transferring the mussels that have cooked to a large bowl, stirring and prodding until all the mussels have opened and have been transferred to the bowl. (Discard any mussels that do not open.) Increase the heat to high and simmer the cider for 3 minutes, or until it has reduced by about a third. Season the liquid to taste with lemon juice and salt, then reduce the heat to low. Return the mussels to the pot, add the crème fraîche and tarragon, and stir gently until the mussels are warmed through and coated with the cream. Serve immediately, with the bread.

celery, kohlrabi, apple, and walnut salad

walnut oil vinaigrette

PREP TIME: 40 MINUTES // TOTAL TIME: 40 MINUTES
SERVES 8 AS PART OF A LARGER MEAL, OR 4 TO 6 WITH A REGULAR DINNER

I LIKE THIS SALAD BECAUSE IT'S an unusual combination of winter produce that's sweet and bitter at the same time, and because its crunchy texture and light, bright flavors act as a good bridge between this menu's mussels and pork, which are both relatively rich.

When you're shopping for kohlrabi, look for baseball-size bulbs with bright-green leaves. To prepare them, first break off the leaves where they attach to the bulb, then cut off the tough root end. Peel the light-green skin off the root with a heavy-duty peeler or a small, sharp knife.

It's easiest to cut the kohlrabi into matchstick-size pieces with a mandoline, but if you don't have one, first cut it into ⅛-inch rounds, then slice the rounds into matchsticks a few at a time. Ditto for the pear: it's much easier to cut paper-thin on a mandoline and the results are beautiful (see My Favorite Tools, page 14), but a good sharp knife will do.

for the SALAD:
2 tablespoons kosher salt
6 stalks celery, from the heart
   of the bunch, cut into ¼-inch
   diagonal slices
3 baseball-size kohlrabi (about
   1¼ pounds total)
1 Bosc pear or sweet-tart apple,
   such as Honeycrisp, halved,
   cored, and cut into paper-thin
   slices
½ cup loosely packed celery leaves
   (just the pale-green inside
   leaves)
½ cup loosely packed parsley leaves
   (no stems)

1 cup whole walnuts, toasted (see
   Toasting Nuts, page 12)
Flaky sea salt, such as Maldon or
   Jacobsen (see Resources, page
   293)

for the VINAIGRETTE:
Big pinch of kosher salt
1 teaspoon Dijon mustard
2 tablespoons apple cider vinegar
   (see Resources, page 293)
½ cup toasted walnut oil (see
   Resources, page 293)
¼ cup extra-virgin olive oil

✦ Bring a small pot of water to a boil and prepare an ice bath. Add 2 tablespoons of the kosher salt, then the celery, and cook for 10 seconds. Drain the celery and plunge it into the ice bath until cool, then drain it again and lay it out on a towel to dry.

✦ Next, peel the kohlrabi and cut it into ⅛-inch-thick matchsticks. If you'd like to make the salad ahead, put the celery and kohlrabi into a mixing bowl, cover with a damp paper towel, and refrigerate for up to 6 hours before serving.

✦ Make the vinaigrette: In a small bowl, whisk the salt together with the mustard and vinegar. Mix the oils together in a measuring cup, then add them to the vinegar mixture in a slow, steady stream, whisking as you go, mixing until the oil is completely incorporated. Set aside.

✦ Just before serving, combine the celery, kohlrabi, pear, celery and parsley leaves, walnuts, and reserved vinaigrette in a large bowl. Toss the ingredients together until everything is well coated, season to taste with flaky sea salt, then pile onto plates and serve.

braised pork shoulder

served crispy with pork demi

PREP TIME: 1 HOUR 45 MINUTES // TOTAL TIME: ABOUT 10 HOURS, OR OVERNIGHT

SERVES 8, WITH LEFTOVERS

SPECIAL EQUIPMENT: 14 (3-FOOT-LONG) PIECES KITCHEN STRING

FOR THE NORMANDY DINNER, WE START with about fifty pounds of pork shoulder. One by one, we butterfly the shoulders, rub them inside and out with salt and pepper, roll them up, and tie them into tight little bundles. Braised in a simple mixture of wine and aromatics, then sliced and pan-fried in olive oil, the shoulders turn into a Norman version of *carnitas*, or refried Mexican-style pork shoulder. (In fact, I always make sure there's enough for tacos the next day.) Once the braising sauce is cooked down to a shiny glaze, we serve the pork with the glaze drizzled on top, over a bed of Braised Cabbage (page 245), with a side of steamed baby white potatoes dressed with crunchy salt, plenty of butter, and finely chopped fresh parsley.

You'll need to either cook the pork the day before you plan to serve it or very early the morning of the party; both the pork and the braising liquid need time to chill completely after they come out of the oven.

NOTE: If you're not comfortable cutting a pork shoulder so it lies flat and is about 1 inch thick, a method called butterflying, ask your butcher to do it for you.

---

2 (4-pound) pork shoulders, butterflied

Kosher salt and freshly ground black pepper

1¼ cups extra-virgin olive oil, divided

6 garlic cloves, smashed and peeled

2 stalks celery, roughly chopped

2 medium carrots, peeled and roughly chopped

2 fresh bay leaves

4 cups dry white wine, divided

4 cups chicken stock, divided

1 yellow onion, peeled and quartered

Braised Cabbage (page 245)

Flaky sea salt, such as Maldon or Jacobsen (see Resources, page 293), for finishing

✦ Spread one pork shoulder out on a cutting board so it lies flat, then season it liberally on both sides with kosher salt and pepper. Starting from one short end, roll the meat up into a tight spiral, turning it seam side down on the board. Using kitchen string, tie the pork tightly at roughly 1-inch intervals, tucking any stray meat under the strings so it is in as compact a bundle as possible. (The tighter the roll, the easier the pork is to handle and the prettier it is once it's braised and seared.)

continued

+ Heat a large, heavy-bottomed soup pot or Dutch oven over medium-high heat. When the pan is hot, add ¼ cup of the olive oil, then the meat, and cook until brown on all sides, turning the meat only when it releases easily from the pan, 10 to 15 minutes total.

+ Season and tie the second roast. When the first shoulder is well browned, transfer it to a large, high-sided roasting pan and repeat the searing process with the second roast, then transfer the second roast to the pan with the first.

+ Preheat the oven to 350 degrees F.

+ Carefully pour the hot oil out of the pot and discard, then add the garlic, celery, carrots, bay leaves, 2 cups of the wine, 2 cups of the stock, and the onion. Bring to a simmer, then cook for 5 minutes, until the onion begins to soften. Transfer the vegetables to the roasting pan with the pork, then pour the hot liquid over them. Add enough of the remaining 2 cups wine and 2 cups stock, in equal parts, to make the liquid come about two-thirds of the way up the sides of the pork. (The amount of liquid you use will depend on the size of your pan.)

+ Place a roasting pan–size piece of parchment paper directly on the surface of the liquid and meat, then cover the pan with aluminum foil, sealing it tightly around the edges to prevent any steam from escaping. Cook the meat for 2½ hours, or until totally tender. Carefully transfer the meat to a serving plate, cover, and refrigerate. Strain the braising liquid into a large bowl and discard the vegetables. Refrigerate the liquid as well, for at least 6 hours, or overnight. (You want the pork to solidify so it becomes sliceable, and the liquid to separate, so you can scoop the fat right off the top.)

+ To serve, preheat the oven to 300 degrees F.

+ Skim all the fat off the surface of the braising liquid, discard it, and transfer the liquid to a small saucepan. Bring it to a hard simmer over medium-high heat and cook, stirring occasionally, until the liquid has reduced to about ½ cup, or until it looks syrupy when you turn the heat off and let the sauce sit for a minute or two, 20 to 30 minutes total.

+ Meanwhile, remove the strings from the pork roasts and cut each into 1-inch slabs. Heat two large ovenproof skillets over medium-high heat. When the pans are hot, add ½ cup oil to each, then add the pork pieces. Cook, undisturbed, for 4 to 5 minutes, or until well browned. Gently turn the pieces over and cook for another 3 to 4 minutes, until browned on the second side. Transfer the pork slices to a large, rimmed baking sheet and repeat with the remaining pork pieces in one of the pans. Transfer the baking sheet to the oven to keep warm for up to 10 minutes—you want the pork to be crisp and brown on both sides and warmed through.

+ Serve the pork immediately over the braised cabbage, drizzled with the sauce and sprinkled with sea salt.

braised cabbage

apples, caraway, cream

PREP TIME: 15 MINUTES // TOTAL TIME: 2 HOURS // SERVES 8

SAVOY CABBAGE, WHOSE CRIMPED, LEATHERY FOLDS make the big, unwieldy heads look like cartoon versions of themselves, are a staple of Normandy's fall and winter cuisine. Spread out on a cutting board, the leaves have a lot in common with tree leaves, with veins running every which way. As beautiful as they are raw, it's worth cooking them; stewed in cider with caraway, cream, and a pinch of spice, they make a perfect bed for a crisp round of the Braised Pork Shoulder (page 243).

¼ cup (½ stick) unsalted butter
1 (2- to 2½- pound) savoy
  cabbage, quartered, cored, and
  sliced into ¼-inch ribbons
2 sweet-tart apples, such as
  Honeycrisp, peeled, halved,
  cored, and thinly sliced
1 tablespoon toasted caraway
  seeds (see Toasting Spices,
  page 13)

1 tablespoon kosher salt, plus more
  for seasoning
½ teaspoon red pepper flakes
Freshly ground black pepper, for
  seasoning
1 (750-milliliter) bottle dry hard
  cider
1 cup heavy cream

+ In a large soup pot or Dutch oven, melt the butter over medium heat. Add the cabbage, apples, caraway seeds, 1 tablespoon of the salt, red pepper flakes, and pepper to taste, and stir to combine. (If there's too much cabbage for your pot, wait a few minutes; the cabbage will shrink as it cooks and you'll be able to add more eventually.) Cover the pot and cook for a few minutes, until the cabbage begins to soften. Add the cider, stir to combine, and bring to a boil. Reduce the heat and cook at a bare bubble for 1½ hours. (The cabbage can be cooked up to this point, removed from the heat, and left at room temperature for up to 4 hours.)

+ About 15 minutes before serving, stir in the cream. Simmer on low heat until the liquid has thickened a bit, about 10 minutes, then season to taste with additional salt, if necessary. Serve hot.

french apple cake

PREP TIME: 45 MINUTES // TOTAL TIME: 3 HOURS // SERVES 8
SPECIAL EQUIPMENT: 9-INCH FLUTED TART PAN WITH A REMOVABLE BOTTOM,
OR 9-INCH PIE PLATE

UNLIKE TRADITIONAL AMERICAN APPLE PIES, THIS one has a filling that focuses solely on the apples; there's no flour to bind them together, so the flavor is, in my opinion, more pure. It's like a pie with a cookie crust, really, which means it's much more forgiving. Be sure to let it sit for a few minutes before slicing—an hour or two is really best—so the cake firms up a bit.

While you're waiting, you should probably drink. In Normandy, drinking calvados, or apple brandy, as a digestif is as much a part of a nice meal as cheese and dessert. Snuggled behind crocks and baking dishes in any good antiques store in the region, you'll find a collection of miniature tulip-shaped wineglasses called *petits pointus*. They're the traditional calvados vessels, and when they come around after a big meal with your *café*, it's wise to take one. Sip slowly, and as the calvados warms your belly, you'll learn why they call it *le trou Normand*, or "the Norman hole"—it makes just enough room for dessert. I love to serve a calvados made by Adrien Camut (see Resources, page 293).

¾ cup (1½ sticks) unsalted butter, softened
1¾ cups sugar, divided
7 large egg yolks, divided
3 cups (about 384 grams) all-purpose flour, plus more for rolling out the dough
⅜ teaspoon baking powder
¼ teaspoon kosher salt

Grated zest and juice of 1 large lemon
5 medium-size tart baking apples (about 2½ pounds total), such as Gravenstein, Pippin, or Granny Smith
3 tablespoons heavy cream, plus more for serving

✦ In the work bowl of a stand mixer fitted with the paddle attachment, cream the butter and 1½ cups of the sugar on medium speed for about a minute, until light and fluffy. Add 6 of the egg yolks a few at a time, mixing well after each addition and stopping the mixer to scrape down the sides of the bowl if necessary.

✦ In a bowl, whisk together the flour, baking powder, and salt, then, with the mixer on low speed, add the dry ingredients in 3 additions, mixing until just combined each time. (The dough will resemble cookie dough more than pie dough.)

✦ Divide the dough into 2 pieces, one twice as big as the other. Place each hunk of dough on a sheet of parchment or waxed paper, press it into a disk, wrap it in plastic wrap, and refrigerate until almost firm, about 1 hour. (If you chill the dough overnight, let it sit at room temperature for 10 to 15 minutes before rolling it out.)

continued

✦ Meanwhile, in a large bowl, whisk the remaining ¼ cup sugar with the lemon zest and set aside. Fill a large bowl with cold water and add the lemon juice to the water. (This will prevent the apples from browning.)

✦ Peel and halve the apples, core them, and cut each half into ¼-inch-thick slices, placing the sliced apples into the lemon water as you go. Set aside.

✦ Working on a lightly floured surface with a floured rolling pin, gently roll out the larger piece of dough to ¼ inch thick and cut it into a circle about 2 inches wider all around than a 9-inch tart pan (or similar pan). Fit the crust into the pan, tucking it carefully into the corners and allowing the extra dough to drape over the edges. Drain the apples well, toss them in the bowl with the sugar and lemon zest, and pile them into the tart pan so they make a tall mound in the middle. Use your wet hands to pat a little moisture onto the bottom crust where it rests on the edge of the tart pan. Roll out the smaller piece of dough to ¼ inch thick, and drape it over the top of the apples, gently pressing it into the moist part of the bottom crust without stretching it too much on top. Once the dough is draped all the way around, with the extra dough hanging over the pan's edges, effectively sealing the apples in, use your fingers to press the dough down into the sharp edge of the tart pan, separating the cake from the extra dough. (There should be a good inch of extra dough all the way around that gets trimmed off by the edge of the tart pan when you press your fingers into it.) If the top hasn't cracked naturally, cut a few vents into it.

✦ Place the cake on a baking sheet and chill for 1 hour.

✦ Preheat the oven to 350 degrees F.

✦ In a small bowl, whisk together the remaining egg yolk and the 3 tablespoons cream. Brush the crust all over with the cream mixture, then bake (on the baking sheet) for 60 to 70 minutes, until the top is golden brown, rotating the tart after about 40 minutes. Let sit at least 30 minutes before slicing and serving, with extra warm cream poured over.

CIDER

Hard cider is having a renaissance in the United States. Traditionally, American cider has been sweeter, so chefs looking to cook with cider have turned to England, France, and Spain for drier varieties. Today, though, American producers, like Washington's Finnriver Farm & Cidery, are making farmstead and craft ciders that pair extremely well with food, both for cooking and for drinking. Given our state's geography and climate—one quite similar to Normandy's, perfect for growing apples and pears—it seems natural for cider to become increasingly popular in the Pacific Northwest.

Wood Oven Dinner

Roasted Marrow Bones *253*
Rye Toasts, Parsley and Caper Salad

Roasted Chicken *257*
Fried Capers, Preserved Lemon

Roasted Turnips *259*
Brown Butter Vinaigrette, Marjoram

Roasted Carrots and Fennel *263*
Yogurt, Harissa

Zucchini Bread *267*
Crème Fraîche, Sea Salt

SERVES 4

IF IT WERE ACCEPTABLE TO WEAR SMOKE as a perfume, I might consider doing it. For me, it's a reminder of traveling in France, where you can walk into a *ferme auberge* and eat food that's fresh off a wood stove in the center of the room. As a society, we have cooked over burning wood for centuries, and for me, it's a big part of the flavor of food. At The Whale Wins, I wanted to replicate the experience of eating in the same room as a fire.

Our oven there, a Mugnaini wood-fired oven, our Italian immigrant, is a living, breathing thing. Around 5 o'clock each morning, when the first cooks arrive, we remove the metal sheet that shuts her up for the night, revealing the coals we've spread across the deck the night before. The residual heat from the previous day leaves the oven at about 350 degrees Fahrenheit overnight, so when we start a new fire with the cords of applewood delivered to our porch every three weeks or so, we're usually starting with a warm oven. We love that the oven changes a little every day, but it also means we change our habits depending on how hot she's running—on most days, somewhere between 580 and 620 degrees Fahrenheit.

Over time, our 6-by-4-foot marble-fronted baby is getting more consistent. As cooks, we're learning its hot spots, and how the air inside rotates differently depending on where we build the fire. It takes practice, but ultimately, the smoky background it gives the restaurant's food can't be mimicked without a 100 percent wood fire.

I assume you won't have an oven like ours, so I've adjusted these recipes to work in a regular home oven. However, note that, as at The Whale Wins, each recipe in this menu starts with a hot pan. You can use a steel pan like we do there or a cast-iron one—just make sure it's completely heatproof and well seasoned.

Serve this menu with a slightly chilled Beaujolais, such as one from Morgon.

roasted marrow bones

rye toasts, parsley and caper salad

PREP TIME: 45 MINUTES // TOTAL TIME: 24 HOURS // SERVES 4

Despite their rather primitive appearance when raw, roasted beef marrow bones are undeniably beautiful, with a remarkably delicate flavor. Serve the bones on a platter, with long, thin marrow spoons, if you can find them. To eat them, dig out the marrow, pile it liberally onto the toasts, and top with the salad.

The overnight brining process achieves two goals; it both preserves the pretty pink color of the bones and makes them easier to clean before roasting. If you prefer, ask your butcher to do the cleaning for you.

If you want to have more shallots on hand, you can use Simplest Pickled Shallots (page 222) and their brine instead of making the small amount needed here for the salad.

Note: At The Whale Wins, we serve marrow bones that are about 4 inches long, or 1 pound each. It's fine to roast any size bones, as long as you cook them until they're completely tender in the center.

---

for the BONES:
2 quarts cold water
½ cup kosher salt
4 beef marrow bones (about
 4 pounds total)

for the SALAD:
½ cup golden raisins
¼ cup brandy
¼ cup dry white wine
3 small shallots, cut into
 ⅛-inch-thick rings
½ cup champagne vinegar (see
 Resources, page 293)
½ cup salt-packed capers (salt-
 packed preferred), rinsed well
 (see Capers, page 188)

1 cup roughly chopped fresh
 Italian parsley leaves
Julienned peel of 1 preserved
 lemon (see Using Preserved
 Lemons, page 13)
2 tablespoons extra-virgin olive oil
Crushed flaky sea salt, such
 as Maldon or Jacobsen (see
 Resources, page 293), for
 finishing
Freshly ground black pepper

for serving:
Flaky sea salt, such as Maldon or
 Jacobsen
12 slices Rye Toasts (page 278)

→ Make the brine for the marrow bones: Stir together the water and kosher salt until the salt dissolves. Submerge the bones in the brine and refrigerate overnight.

continued

✦ Next, for the salad, combine the raisins, brandy, and wine in a small saucepan. Bring to a simmer over high heat, remove the pan from the heat, cover it, and set aside at room temperature to infuse the raisins overnight. Combine the shallots and vinegar in a small bowl, cover, and refrigerate overnight.

✦ The next day, about 2 hours before cooking, remove the bones from the brine, pat them dry, and set them on a baking sheet in the refrigerator for about 1 hour to dry further. When they are dry, use the back of a sharp paring knife to scrape the sinew and fat off the sides of all the bones. (You may also find a metal bench scraper, the kind meant for baking, to be useful here. It's okay if you don't get it all, but the cleaner the bones are, the prettier they'll be.)

✦ Preheat the oven to 500 degrees F. Place the bones in a large ovenproof pan and roast for 20 to 30 minutes, or until they are completely soft in the center when stabbed all the way through with a skewer. (It's important that the centers are completely soft, so the marrow is spreadable.)

✦ While the bones roast, make the salad: First, drain the liquid off the raisins and place the raisins in a small mixing bowl. Stir in the pickled shallots, 2 tablespoons of the shallot brine, the capers, parsley, lemon peel, and olive oil. Season to taste with salt and pepper. (If you'd like, reserve the remaining shallot brine for a salad dressing.)

✦ To serve: Transfer the hot bones to a large platter and sprinkle a large pinch of sea salt flakes over the top of each one. Serve immediately, next to the salad and rye toasts.

roasted chicken

fried capers, preserved lemon

PREP TIME: 20 MINUTES // TOTAL TIME: 50 MINUTES // SERVES 4

A WELL-RAISED CHICKEN HAS AN INTERESTING flavor all its own, which is why when we roast them at our restaurants, we use just butter and salt for seasoning. In the wood oven, I especially love how the bottom half of the chicken—the part without the skin—caramelizes against the hot pan.

If you don't feel comfortable taking the back out of a chicken, so the chicken is in two halves, ask your butcher to do it for you. You can also purchase two hindquarters and two breast halves (with the drumettes still attached) if you prefer.

In the fall, we often serve this chicken atop a simple rutabaga and parsnip puree, made by boiling one pound of each vegetable until soft, then pureeing with cream, a bit of water, and a thumb-size chunk of preserved lemon until completely smooth. The puree will serve four as a robust side dish, or you can smear it under the chicken on each plate at a party for eight to ten. You can also serve the chicken with Duck Fat–Fried Potatoes (page 279).

NOTE: You can roast an entire chicken using the same method; tuck the chicken's wings behind its back before roasting, and increase the total roasting time by 10 to 15 minutes, depending on the bird's size.

½ cup capers (salt-packed preferred), rinsed well (see Capers, page 188)
½ cup plus 1 tablespoon extra-virgin olive oil, divided
½ cup (1 stick) unsalted butter
1 (4-pound) chicken, back removed, halves dried 1 hour in the refrigerator, and brined if desired (see Brining Birds, page 258)

1 tablespoon crunchy gray salt (see Resources, page 293)
Julienned peel of 1 preserved lemon (see Using Preserved Lemons, page 13)
Finishing oil, for drizzling

✦ Preheat the oven to 500 degrees F. Place a large, heavy ovenproof skillet on the bottom rack of the oven and let it preheat for 5 minutes.

✦ Put 1 tablespoon of the olive oil and the stick of butter into the hot pan. Return the pan to the oven for a minute or so, until the butter is melted and foamy. Carefully place the chicken pieces into the pan, skin side up. Holding the pan at an angle with an oven mitt, spoon the butter over the chicken, basting it for a full minute, until the butter has run down every possible surface of the pieces. Sprinkle the chicken evenly with the salt, crushing it between your fingers as you go.

continued

✦ Roast the chicken in the hottest part of the oven (bottom right, for most ovens) for 35 to 40 minutes, rotating the pan about halfway through. (Do not turn the chicken over. If your chicken's skin begins to brown before the inside is fully cooked, move it to a cooler section of your oven, tent it with aluminum foil, or place a baking sheet on the rack above it.) The chicken is done when the skin is nicely browned and the thickest part of the biggest piece measures 165 degrees F on an instant-read thermometer.

✦ Set the chicken aside on a cutting board to rest for 5 minutes.

✦ Meanwhile, strain the capers, if needed, and transfer them to a paper towel–lined plate to dry for a moment. Heat the remaining ½ cup olive oil in a small saucepan over high heat. When the oil begins to move in the pan (if you add a caper, it should sizzle ferociously), carefully add the capers, reduce the heat to medium, and fry them until they flower and crisp, 3 to 4 minutes, or more for larger capers. Using a slotted spoon, transfer the capers back to the paper toweling.

✦ Using a sharp knife, separate the hindquarters from the breasts of each chicken. Transfer the chicken to a serving plate and top with the fried capers and lemon peel. Serve warm or at room temperature, drizzled with a great finishing oil.

BRINING BIRDS

We don't brine our chickens at The Whale Wins because, at around 600 degrees F, our wood oven does a great job of searing in juice and flavor. If you'd like to brine yours, heat 1 gallon of water, 1 cup kosher salt, ½ cup sugar, plus a few peppercorns, bay leaves, and chopped celery stalks in a large pot until the salt and sugar dissolve. Cool and chill the brine completely, then submerge the chicken in the brine for about 3 hours, refrigerated. Remove the chicken from the pot and pat it dry, then roast as directed. (If possible, let the chicken dry overnight in the refrigerator, on a cooling rack set over a sheet pan.)

roasted turnips

brown butter vinaigrette, marjoram

PREP TIME: 20 MINUTES, PLUS MAKING THE VINAIGRETTE
TOTAL TIME: 20 MINUTES // SERVES 4

AT THE WHALE WINS, WE USE walnut-size turnips because they're sweet and firm. We also roast them in a hot, hot pan in the wood oven, but at home, it's best to start them on the stovetop, so the flat sides of the halved bulbs get good and toasty. If your turnips come with bright, fresh greens, trim and wash them, and add them to the pan when you put the pan in the oven.

Use the leftover Brown Butter Vinaigrette in place of the butter in the Potato Salad (page 201), or use it in the pan when sautéing vegetables.

NOTE: If you're cooking the menu as a whole, sear and roast the turnips after the chicken comes out of the oven, while the meat rests and the capers fry.

---

2 bunches baby turnips (about ¾ pound), halved, greens trimmed and saved if healthy-looking
1 tablespoon extra-virgin olive oil
½ teaspoon kosher salt

1 tablespoon whole marjoram leaves
¼ cup Brown Butter Vinaigrette (recipe follows)
2 teaspoons freshly squeezed lemon juice

+ Preheat the oven to 500 degrees F.

+ Bring a small saucepan of water to a boil. Add the halved turnips and cook, submerged, for 30 seconds, then drain the turnips and transfer them to a bowl of ice water. When the turnips have cooled completely, drain them and pat them dry on paper towels.

+ Heat a large ovenproof pan over medium-high heat. When hot, add the oil, then the turnips, placing as many cut side down as you can, and cook for 4 to 5 minutes, until they are nicely browned. Carefully turn the turnips over and sprinkle them with the salt and marjoram leaves. Add the vinaigrette and lemon juice to the pan, transfer the pan to the middle rack of the oven, and roast for another 4 to 5 minutes, or until the turnips are tender. Serve warm.

brown butter vinaigrette

PREP TIME: 30 MINUTES // TOTAL TIME: 1 HOUR // MAKES ABOUT ¼ CUP

JAY GUERRERO, THE CHEF AT BOAT Street Café, brought the first version of this recipe to Seattle from his time in New York, where he was the sous chef at Prune. Today, we use it quite often at The Whale Wins. Kept in the refrigerator, it becomes a staple; you can use it wherever you'd use regular butter.

1 cup (2 sticks) unsalted butter
1 small shallot, chopped
Julienned peel of half a preserved
   lemon (see Using Preserved
   Lemons, page 13)

1 teaspoon freshly squeezed lemon
   juice
Kosher salt

✦ Place the butter in a small, heavy saucepan over high heat. When it melts, reduce the heat to medium, and cook until the butter foams, then the foam disappears and the butter begins to brown on the bottom of the pan, about 15 minutes. (You want the tasty bits on the bottom of the pan to be a lovely brown color, but not black.) Pour the butter through a fine-mesh strainer and allow it to cool for about 30 minutes.

✦ In the work bowl of a food processor or heavy-duty blender, whirl the shallot and the lemon peel and juice until finely chopped. With the motor running, slowly add the butter through the top of the machine, and process until almost smooth. Season to taste with salt. Use warm or at room temperature. To store, let the butter cool to room temperature, then refrigerate it, covered, for up to 3 weeks.

roasted carrots and fennel

yogurt, harissa

PREP TIME: 15 MINUTES // TOTAL TIME: 40 TO 45 MINUTES // SERVES 4 TO 6

THIS ROASTED VEGETABLE DISH, WHICH WE always serve at room temperature, depends on the flavor of a bright, rose-scented harissa, like our Rose Petal Harissa (page 282). This is the kind of dish wandering hands can't seem to resist in the hours before a dinner party, while the vegetables wait for the other dishes to cook, so this recipe makes plenty.

NOTE: Be sure to space the vegetables evenly on the baking sheet; you want them to crisp and brown, not steam.

---

2 bunches medium carrots (6-inch carrots, about ¾ pound), trimmed but not peeled, halved lengthwise

2 medium fennel bulbs, cut into ½-inch-thick slices through the core

6 tablespoons extra-virgin olive oil, divided, plus more if needed

1 tablespoon crunchy gray salt (see Resources, page 293)

¼ cup store-bought harissa or Rose Petal Harissa (page 282)

Flaky sea salt, such as Maldon or Jacobsen (see Resources, page 293), for finishing

1½ cups Homemade Yogurt (page 286), plain European-style whole milk yogurt, or Greek yogurt thinned with a bit of olive oil

Finishing oil, for drizzling

+ Preheat the oven to 500 degrees F.

+ Arrange the carrots and fennel on a large, rimmed baking sheet. Drizzle the vegetables with 4 tablespoons of the olive oil, turning to coat, then sprinkle with the gray salt. Roast for 30 to 35 minutes, rotating the pan and turning the vegetables halfway through, until the vegetables are tender and well browned on the bottom.

+ Allow the vegetables to cool to room temperature. In a large bowl, blend the remaining 2 tablespoons olive oil with the harissa. (If your harissa is especially thick, you may need another tablespoon or two of oil, just so it's thin enough to coat the vegetables.) Add the vegetables, turn to coat them evenly with the harissa mixture, and season to taste with the sea salt.

+ To serve, smear the yogurt on a serving plate. Pile the vegetables on top, and serve at room temperature, drizzled with finishing oil.

THE STAFF

I grew up in Boat Street Café. When I took over its operation in April of 1998, there were only about a dozen of us. I was the same age as most of my employees, so they quickly became my family. Of course, my family was there also. My dad was in the kitchen with me, asking me the same questions over and over again, trying to soak it all in. My mom waited tables. I remember her racing back into the kitchen with a bottle of wine on the very first night, panicked because she didn't know how to open it with a waiter's corkscrew.

From the beginning, I knew that when I hire someone, I'm hiring them into our family—perhaps precisely because at first, I was quite literally working with my family. I have developed deep friendships with the people I hired at Boat Street over a decade ago, and today, still, I look for people I can imagine spending time with when the restaurant doors close. It's a challenge to be someone's boss and friend at the same time, but some of the most remarkable experiences— good and bad—have happened because I'm so close to the people I work with.

I also look for staff who aren't just like me. Hiring someone with different strengths helps make me more well rounded as a person and as a cook. I'm attracted to creative minds, so many Boat Streeters, as we called ourselves before our other restaurants opened, are artists outside the restaurant life— up-and-coming painters or sculptors, or people whose careers simply require a second income. Ultimately, it means we're a group of really dynamic people who bring color and creativity to the restaurants. I think we could make a lot of money selling tickets to our holiday parties, because as a whole, we're a pretty entertaining crowd.

In the kitchen, I like to focus on the fact that I'm never really done learning. My staff make fun of me for choosing the tedious tasks at work. I love peeling the bones out of anchovies, or cleaning squid, or scraping barnacles off oysters because it allows me to stand in one spot and meditate on a task that can actually be finished. Nowadays, it also allows me to watch what my chefs are doing. They're always teaching me.

Sometimes when people give me credit for running this business, I want to roll my eyes. Sure, I'm the one who hauls myself out of bed if someone breaks into the kitchen at 4 a.m., but the staff keep our tables filled day in and day out, doing everything from chopping and dishwashing to serving and pouring wine. I'm no longer the one who repaints the toe kick under the white cabinets. I don't usually stack wood at The Whale Wins. As I see it, my job now is to find people I love working with, and to trust them.

continued

Eli Dahlin, the original head chef at The Walrus and the Carpenter, is someone I hired at Boat Street Café years ago. Over the years, we developed a bond. He's dedicated and endlessly creative, so when we, as a team, started thinking about opening Walrus, as we call it, I knew he was my guy; I wanted an evolving menu inspired by the Puget Sound. He's the kind of cook that looks at salmon skin—something some of us might see as trash—and crisps it into salmon chips dusted with salt and piment d'Espelette. He's a brilliant culinary mind.

Marie Rutherford started working with me in 2008. She and I have lived oddly similar lives; we both went through art school with a vision of ourselves as artists and teachers, and ended up cooking immediately after graduation, without any formal training. When Russell Flint (see Profile, page 35) left Boat Street Café, she came to run the kitchen in his stead. We opened The Whale Wins together in 2012. It was as if the concept had been tailored to fit her; she'd spent time in Normandy and knew her way around a wood-fired oven. She echoes my love for classic French style and is responsible for maintaining Whale's distinctively French accent. Marie is dependable and creative, and hysterically funny when the kitchen needs it most.

Jay Guerrero started at Boat Street in 2012, but it's as if he's been here for ten years. When Marie moved to The Whale Wins, I worried about stealing her from Boat Street, because I didn't want to take away something that made it great. But serendipity rules: just as I began looking for someone I trusted, Gabrielle Hamilton, the owner and chef at Prune in New York City, wrote recommending Jay. Since he grew up and spent time cooking in a food culture very much like mine, I knew I wouldn't have to edit his cooking, which was crucial to me. He fit perfectly; today, he's an integral part of our team. He's charismatic and funny, and he can walk into any room and make friends.

Bobby Palmquist doesn't look like a chef. When he started working for me, he had little to no experience cooking in restaurants, and he cooked like he runs—much, much faster than any human should. But since the beginning, he's had an infectious enthusiasm that has made him a good leader. After a few years at The Whale Wins and Boat Street Café, I chose him to lead the kitchen at Barnacle. I rely on Bobby to dive into any new project, and to constantly teach himself more about food and food history, and then turn around and teach it to the rest of us. (He's also a good dog walker.)

In the summer of 2009—one of the hottest on record in Seattle—there was a stretch of 100-degree days in early August when we refused to turn on the ovens. We sweltered. We drank rosé and joked that Boat Street was our place of refuge. It was where we'd all go to die, if the apocalypse came.

But in the end, it's not really a joke. My restaurants are my refuge. The staff are the people I want with me in the toughest of times. They're the backbone of my business, but they're also my life. For their minds and hard work, their inspiration and dedication and friendship, I am eternally grateful.

zucchini bread

crème fraîche, sea salt

PREP TIME: 30 MINUTES // TOTAL TIME: 1 HOUR 40 MINUTES // SERVES 8
SPECIAL EQUIPMENT: 9-BY-5-INCH LOAF PAN

ENRICHED WITH EXTRA-VIRGIN OLIVE OIL AND scented with nutmeg, ginger, and lemon zest, this probably isn't your grandmother's zucchini bread. At The Whale Wins, we toast it in the wood oven in plenty of butter and dust it with Jacobsen sea salt, but you can also eat it warm from the oven, or however you see fit.

for the BREAD:
3 cups grated zucchini (from
    1 pound zucchini)
2 cups granulated sugar, divided
Unsalted butter, for the pan
2 cups (about 256 grams)
    all-purpose flour, sifted,
    plus more for the pan
2 teaspoons ground ginger
1 teaspoon baking powder
½ teaspoon baking soda
½ teaspoon freshly grated nutmeg
3 large eggs

Grated zest from 2 large lemons
2 teaspoons vanilla extract
1 cup extra-virgin olive oil
2 tablespoons demerara sugar (see
    Resources, page 293)

for serving:
Unsalted butter
Crème fraîche
Flaky sea salt, such as Maldon or
    Jacobsen (see Resources,
    page 293)

+ Preheat the oven to 350 degrees F.

+ Make the bread: In a mixing bowl, blend the zucchini with ¼ cup of the granulated sugar. Transfer the mixture to a fine-mesh strainer and set the strainer over the mixing bowl. Fill another bowl, this one just big enough to fit inside the strainer, about halfway with water and carefully set the water bowl directly on top of the zucchini. (This process presses the water out of the zucchini.)

+ Butter and flour a 9-by-5-inch loaf pan, and set aside.

+ In a medium bowl, whisk together the flour, ginger, baking powder, baking soda, and nutmeg.

+ In another bowl, whisk together the remaining 1¾ cups granulated sugar, eggs, lemon zest, and vanilla until well blended. Beat in the olive oil in three stages, whisking until it is thoroughly combined each time.

continued

+ Gently fold the dry ingredients into the wet ingredients until no white spots remain. Working with a handful of zucchini at a time, use your hands to press and wring all excess moisture out of the zucchini. When all the zucchini has been pressed, add it to the batter, and stir it in gently until evenly distributed.

+ Pour the batter into the prepared pan and sprinkle the top evenly with the demerara sugar. Bake on the middle rack of the oven for 70 to 75 minutes, or until a skewer inserted into the center of the loaf comes out clean.

+ Cool the bread in the pan for about 20 minutes, then turn it out onto a cooling rack and let it cool completely.

+ To serve: Cut the bread into 1-inch-thick slabs. Melt about 3 tablespoons of butter in a large skillet over medium heat. (Use the same amount of butter for however many pieces of bread will fit into the skillet at once.) When the butter is melted and foamy, add a few slices, and cook for a few minutes on each side, until warm and toasted. Serve the bread over a smear of crème fraîche, sprinkled with sea salt. Repeat with the remaining bread.

❧ Fall Ingredients ❧

APPLES

Apple Pie with Shirlee's Crust

✦ Peel and core **7 medium tart apples** (about 3½ pounds) and cut each apple into 8 wedges. In a mixing bowl, stir together the apples with the **grated zest and juice of 1 large lemon**, **½ teaspoon kosher salt**, and **1 cup sugar**. Pile the apples into a pie plate lined with **Shirlee's Crust** (page 290), top with the second crust, pinch the edges closed, cut vents in the top, brush with **cream**, dust with **sugar**, and bake at 350 degrees F for 1 to 1½ hours, or until the crust is deep golden brown. *Makes 1.*

Applesauce with Butter and Black Pepper

✦ Peel and core **2 pounds tart apples** (about 4) and cut them into ½-inch wedges. In a saucepan, stir together the apples, **½ cup sugar**, and a **pinch of salt**. Cook the apples over medium-low heat, covered, stirring occasionally, until they are soft and falling apart and the mixture is starting to darken. Mash in **2 tablespoons unsalted butter**, a grinding of **black pepper**, and **1 tablespoon of calvados or cognac**. Serve with the crêpes from Gâteau de Crêpes (page 78). *Makes about 2 cups.*

Baked Apples

✦ Dig the core out of **4 large tart apples** with a melon baller, leaving a 1-inch hole that goes almost all the way to the bottom of each apple. Put the apples in a baking dish. Stir together **1 cup walnuts, finely chopped**, with **½ stick melted butter**, **¼ cup packed dark brown sugar**, and **½ teaspoon ground cinnamon**. Stuff the walnut mixture into the apples and bake at 350 degrees F until the apples are soft all the way through, 45 minutes to 1 hour. Serve warm, with **heavy cream** poured over. *Serves 4.*

BRUSSELS SPROUTS

Deep-Fried Brussels Sprouts with Salt, Chives, and Piment d'Espelette

✦ Halve (or quarter, if large) **1 pound brussels sprouts** and blanch in boiling salted water for 2 minutes, then transfer to a paper towel–lined sheet pan to dry. In a large soup pot, heat about **3 inches canola oil** until it measures 335 degrees F on an instant-read thermometer. Fry the sprouts in small batches for 4 minutes per batch, or until deeply browned, letting the oil come up to temperature between each batch. Transfer the hot sprouts to a paper towel–lined plate and season generously with flaky sea salt, chopped chives, and piment d'Espelette (see Resources, page 293). Serve hot. *Serves 4.*

Raw Shaved Brussels Sprouts with Apples, Walnut Oil, and Black Pepper

✦ In a serving bowl, toss together 1 pound trimmed, shaved brussels sprouts with 1 thinly sliced Honeycrisp apple, ¼ cup champagne vinegar, ½ cup walnut oil, flaky sea salt, and a big grinding of black pepper. *Serves 6 to 8.*

Roasted Brussels Sprouts Carbonara with Cayenne

✦ Halve (or quarter, if large) ¾ pound brussels sprouts, blanch in boiling salted water for 4 minutes, then drain. Heat a large ovenproof skillet over high heat. Add 1 tablespoon each butter and olive oil, swirl to melt, then add the blanched sprouts. Season with salt and toss to coat with the butter and oil. Turn the sprouts cut side down, reduce the heat to medium, and cook them another 6 to 8 minutes, shaking the pan occasionally, or until browned on all sides. Meanwhile, cook ½ pound spaghetti according to package instructions, reserving 1 cup pasta water as the spaghetti cooks. In a serving bowl, whisk together 2 large egg yolks, ½ cup cream, and a pinch of cayenne pepper (or to taste) to blend, then add in the hot pasta, ¼ pound chopped cooked bacon (if desired), and as much reserved water as necessary to coat the noodles with the cream. Add 2 cups freshly grated Parmesan cheese and the sprouts, and toss to mix. *Serves 2 to 4.*

EGGPLANT

Caviar d'Aubergine

✦ Brush the cut sides of 2 large (1-pound) eggplant with about 1 tablespoon olive oil, arrange them face down on a parchment-lined baking sheet, and roast until they're so soft they collapse, 30 to 45 minutes. Let the cooked eggplants cool to room temperature, then peel. Pulse the flesh in a food processor with 2 tablespoons freshly squeezed lemon juice, 1 teaspoon toasted ground cumin, 1 clove minced garlic, and kosher salt to taste until the flesh is finely chopped. With the machine on, drizzle in ½ cup extra-virgin olive oil and whirl just until incorporated. Serve smeared on Grilled Bread (page 277). *Makes about 3 cups.*

Eggplant with Walnut-Parsley Pesto

✦ Make the **Mint and Parsley Pesto** (from the Raw Asparagus Salad recipe on page 116), substituting **toasted walnuts** for the pine nuts and more **parsley** for the mint. Cut a **large (1-pound) eggplant** into ¾-inch-thick rounds, toss with **2 tablespoons olive oil**, season with **kosher salt**, and roast on a parchment-lined baking sheet in a 400-degree F oven until browned and soft, about 30 minutes, then let cool slightly. Smear ½ cup of the pesto on a serving plate, top with the eggplant, and serve at room temperature, drizzled with **finishing oil** and **flaky sea salt**. *Serves 4.*

Pickled Baby Eggplant

✦ Follow the recipe for Pickled Fennel (page 213), substituting **2 pounds trimmed, halved, golf ball–size eggplant** for the fennel, omitting the orange peel, and adding **2 teaspoons whole toasted cumin seed**. (You'll need to weight the eggplant with a small plate as it cooks.) *Makes 3 pints.*

PEARS

Bosc Pear, Radicchio, and Walnut Salad

✦ Very thinly slice a **½-pound head radicchio**, and arrange on a platter. Just before serving, top with **1 very thinly sliced ripe Bosc pear**, **1 cup toasted walnuts** (crushed), **¼ cup picked fresh Italian parsley leaves**, **½ cup walnut oil**, and **¼ cup freshly squeezed lemon juice**. Season with **salt**, toss to distribute the oil and lemon juice evenly, check for seasoning, and serve immediately. *Serves 6 to 8.*

Pear and Roquefort Toasts

✦ Layer a dozen **Baguette Toasts** (page 278) with **4 ounces thinly sliced Roquefort cheese** and bake for 3 to 5 minutes at 350 degrees F, until melted and crisp. (The cheese will melt off into the pan and brown.) Top with very thin slices of **1 Comice pear** and a touch of **flaky sea salt**. *Serves 4.*

Poached Pears with Lemon Peel, Fresh Bay, and Peppercorns

✦ In a medium saucepan, combine **1 bottle dry unoaked white wine** (such as a Côtes de Gascogne) with **1 cup water**, **½ cup sugar**, the **stripped peel of 1 lemon**, **2 fresh bay leaves**, and **3 black peppercorns**. Bring the mixture to a simmer, stirring until the sugar has dissolved, then add **4 peeled, halved, and cored firm-ripe Bosc pears**. Cover and cook, turning the pears occasionally, until they are completely soft when poked with a skewer, 10 to 20 minutes. (Cooking time will depend on the size and ripeness of your pears.) Transfer the pears to a serving platter, increase the heat to high, and boil the cooking liquid until it has reduced to a syrup, about 30 minutes. Serve the pears at room temperature, drizzled with the syrup, with a scoop of **lightly sweetened whipped cream or crème fraîche**. *Serves 4.*

RADICCHIO

Baked Radicchio with Cream

✦ Cut a ¾-pound **radicchio head** into 8 wedges through the core, leaving the core intact. Arrange the slices in a gratin dish just large enough to fit them all, then sprinkle with the **julienned peel of 1 small lemon**. Drizzle **¾ cup cream** over the radicchio, season with **salt**, and bake at 350 degrees F for about 45 minutes, basting once or twice, until the cream has reduced almost all the way and the radicchio is beginning to brown. *Serves 4.*

Radicchio and Comté Cheese Tart

✦ Cut a ¾-**pound head radicchio** into ¼-inch-thick rounds, removing any core bits. In a large skillet over medium heat, melt **2 tablespoons butter**. Add the radicchio and cook, stirring occasionally, until it wilts, about 5 minutes. Set aside, and cook **¼ pound bacon cubes** until browned, then drain the bacon on a paper towel–lined plate. In a mixing bowl, whisk together **3 large eggs, 1 cup heavy cream, 1 teaspoon Dijon mustard, 1 teaspoon fresh thyme leaves, ½ teaspoon kosher salt**, and a generous grating of **fresh nutmeg**. In a tart pan lined with **Shirlee's Crust** (page 290), layer the cooked radicchio, bacon, and **1 cup grated Comté cheese**, then pour the egg mixture on top. Place the pan on a baking sheet and bake at 350 degrees F for about 45 minutes, or until set in the center and golden brown around the edges. *Serves 6 to 8.*

Simple Grilled Radicchio

✦ Cut a ¾-**pound head radicchio** into 8 wedges through the core, leaving the core intact. Drizzle **2 tablespoons extra-virgin olive oil** over the radicchio, smearing it on both sides, then grill the radicchio over high heat for about 4 minutes, until browned and soft on both sides, turning once. Season with **flaky sea salt** and **the juice of half a medium lemon**, drizzle with **the oil**, dust with **2 tablespoons grated Parmesan cheese**, and serve warm or at room temperature. *Serves 4.*

Staples

JUST AS ANYONE DOES, I have a core group of recipes I rely on, both in my restaurants and at home, on a regular basis. From simple toasts to homemade dairy products, these are the things I take the time to make myself.

homemade bread crumbs

PREP TIME: 10 MINUTES // TOTAL TIME: 30 MINUTES // MAKES 1¼ CUPS

THE PERFECT BREAD CRUMBS ADD TWO things: texture and flavor. And while store-bought bread crumbs might get the former just right, they almost always lack the latter, which is why I make my own.

These bread crumbs freeze well; just make sure you let them cool completely before you pack them into an airtight package and slip them into the freezer. The recipe doubles easily as well, but you'll probably need to whirl the bread in a few different batches.

½ day-old baguette, torn into 2-inch pieces	2 tablespoons unsalted butter, cut into 4 pieces
1 teaspoon fresh thyme leaves	½ teaspoon kosher salt

✦ Preheat the oven to 350 degrees F.

✦ In the work bowl of a food processor, whirl the bread chunks until they've broken into marble-size pieces. (You might need to do this in 2 or 3 batches, depending on the size of your bowl.)

✦ Spread the bread out on a baking sheet and bake for 15 to 20 minutes, or until the bread is dry and browned, rotating the pan once or twice during baking.

✦ Transfer the toasty pieces back to the food processor, add the thyme, butter, and salt, and pulse until the crumbs are finely ground.

✦ Transfer the crumbs back to the baking sheet to cool, then store in an airtight container at room temperature for up to 3 days before using, or freeze for up to 3 months.

grilled bread

PREP TIME: 10 MINUTES // TOTAL TIME: 15 MINUTES // SERVES 4

BECAUSE THE CRUST ON A LOAF of great fresh bread should be savored, I always use a day-old loaf for this simple side dish. The purpose of cooking bread this way—until it's well past toasty, and the edges have been charred to a deep, dark brown—is to achieve a flavor that's much stronger than toast's. Top the grilled bread to make tartines, dip it into soups, or serve it as is, sprinkled with flaky sea salt. Seattle isn't exactly known for sun, so when it's too chilly to grill, I often make this at home in a cast-iron grill pan.

For thinner toasts—anything where the bread will be served as stand-up bites, rather than used to mop things up off a plate—cut the bread into ½-inch-thick slices instead.

1 large loaf artisanal bread or baguette, cut into ¾-inch-thick slices

Extra-virgin olive oil (about ¼ cup for a baguette, more for larger loaves)

Flaky sea salt, such as Maldon or Jacobsen (see Resources, page 293), for finishing

✦ Prepare a charcoal or gas grill for cooking over high heat, about 500 degrees F, or heat a heavy indoor grill pan to smoking hot. Brush the cooking grates clean.

✦ Brush the bread slices on each side with the olive oil (or toss the bread and olive oil together in a bowl, if you prefer), then grill for 1 to 2 minutes per side, weighting the bread down with a big saucepan, kettle, or pot on the second side, to ensure an even char. (If you're cooking indoors, grill the bread one or two pieces at a time.)

✦ When the bread is done, transfer it to a cooling rack until ready to serve. (Stacking the slices will cause them to steam and get soggy.) Sprinkle the slices with the salt and serve, warm or at room temperature.

rye toasts

PREP TIME: 10 MINUTES // TOTAL TIME: 30 MINUTES // MAKES 2 DOZEN

IF YOUR BREAD IS ESPECIALLY SOFT, or if you want consistent-looking slices, freeze it for about an hour before slicing. Bring it to room temperature, cutting thin slices off as soon as the bread is soft enough to cut with a large serrated knife.

Half a large (1½-pound) loaf
   Jewish rye bread, halved again
   lengthwise
3 tablespoons extra-virgin olive oil

Flaky sea salt, such as Maldon or
   Jacobsen (see Resources, page
   293), for finishing

✦ Preheat the oven to 350 degrees F.

✦ Using a large serrated knife, slice the bread very thinly—¼ inch at the thickest, or a bit thinner, if possible. Arrange the slices on 2 large baking sheets, brush with the olive oil, sprinkle with salt to taste, and bake for 15 to 20 minutes, or until the toasts are medium brown and crispy, rotating the pans once or twice during baking. (Toward the end of baking, if the toasts aren't cooking at the same rate, remove the browned ones so you can let the others continue baking.)

✦ Serve immediately, or let cool on a cooling rack and serve within a few hours.

baguette toasts

PREP TIME: 10 MINUTES // TOTAL TIME: 30 MINUTES // MAKES ABOUT 3 DOZEN

SLICED AND DRIZZLED WITH OLIVE OIL, then baked, simple baguette toasts are a staple in my kitchens.

1 baguette (about ¾ pound)
⅓ cup extra-virgin olive oil

Flaky sea salt, such as Maldon or
   Jacobsen (see Resources, page
   293), for finishing

✦ Preheat the oven to 350 degrees F.

✦ Using a large serrated knife, cut the bread diagonally into ½-inch slices. Arrange the slices on 2 large baking sheets, brush with the olive oil, sprinkle with salt to taste, and bake for 10 to 15 minutes, or until the toasts are blonde and crisp, rotating the pans once or twice during baking. (Toward the end of baking, if the toasts aren't cooking at the same rate, remove the browned ones so you can let the others continue baking.)

✦ Serve immediately, or let cool on a cooling rack and serve within a few hours.

duck fat–fried potatoes

PREP TIME: 20 MINUTES // TOTAL TIME: 25 MINUTES // SERVES 4 TO 6

ALTHOUGH DUCK FAT KEEPS FOREVER IN the refrigerator—up to six months, well sealed—you can also use schmaltz, or chicken fat, as a substitute. If you make your own chicken stock, you'll find the schmaltz floating in a thick, buttery yellow cap at the top of the liquid once it's been chilled overnight. Simply scoop it off the top and use it like butter.

½ cup rendered duck fat
1 pound fingerling potatoes,
  halved lengthwise

Flaky sea salt, such as Maldon or
  Jacobsen (see Resources, page
  293), for finishing

✦ Preheat the oven to 450 degrees F.

✦ In a large ovenproof skillet, heat the duck fat over medium-high heat. When it's hot, add the potatoes. Shake the pan to toss them around, covering each potato with the fat. Turn the potatoes cut side down and let them cook for 6 to 8 minutes, turning occasionally, until they're browned on all sides.

✦ Transfer the skillet to the oven and roast the potatoes for 6 to 8 minutes more, until tender.

✦ Transfer the potatoes to a paper towel–lined plate and let them drain, then slide them into a mixing bowl and toss them with plenty of salt. Serve warm.

homemade mayonnaise

PREP TIME: 10 MINUTES // TOTAL TIME: 10 MINUTES // MAKES 1½ CUPS

IF I'M GOING TO USE MAYONNAISE as an ingredient in a sauce or dressing, I use jarred mayonnaise, but if I'm serving it on its own—as an accompaniment to roasted chicken, for example—I make my own. You can make this by hand, whisking the oil into the egg yolk mixture with as much vigor as you can muster and adding it only a very little bit at a time, but I find the food processor does a nice job and saves time and work.

To make tarragon mayonnaise (to substitute for the mayonnaise used in the Crab Melts on page 150), add 1 tablespoon picked tarragon leaves to the food processor and pulse a few times before you begin adding the oil.

NOTE: Since you'll be eating the yolks raw, use the best eggs you can find.

---

2 large egg yolks, at room
   temperature
1 tablespoon freshly squeezed
   lemon juice
2 teaspoons white wine vinegar

½ teaspoon Dijon mustard
1 teaspoon kosher salt
1½ cups canola oil (or a blend of
   canola oil and olive oil)

✦ In the work bowl of a food processor, whirl the egg yolks, lemon juice, vinegar, mustard, and salt until well blended. With the motor running, add the oil in a slow, steady stream through the top of the machine. When all the oil has been added and the mixture is thick, season to taste with additional salt, if necessary, then transfer to a bowl and refrigerate, covered, until ready to use, up to 3 days.

garlic aioli

PREP TIME: 10 MINUTES // TOTAL TIME: 10 MINUTES // MAKES 1½ CUPS

WHERE MAYONNAISE HAS MOSTLY MUSTARD AND vinegar flavors, aioli, though made the same way, is all about the garlic. I love using aioli for fried oysters—especially with a heavy dose of *piment d'Espelette* stirred in—and as a dip for french fries.

You can use a mild extra-virgin olive oil for all of the oil in this recipe, but using just strong olive oil will make the aioli bitter.

NOTE: Since you'll be eating the yolks raw, use the best eggs you can find.

---

2 large egg yolks, at room
  temperature
1 tablespoon freshly squeezed
  lemon juice

1 teaspoon kosher salt
2 garlic cloves, minced
¾ cup extra-virgin olive oil
¾ cup canola oil

✦ In the work bowl of a food processor, whirl the egg yolks, lemon juice, salt, and garlic until well blended. With the machine running, add the oils in a slow, steady stream through the top of the machine. When both oils have been added and the mixture is thick, season to taste with additional salt, if necessary, then transfer to a bowl and refrigerate, covered, until ready to use, up to 3 days.

rose petal harissa

PREP TIME: 35 MINUTES // TOTAL TIME: 24 HOURS // MAKES: 3 PINTS
SPECIAL EQUIPMENT: 3 PINT-SIZE JARS

HARISSA IS A CHILI PASTE COMMON to much of the northern half of Africa, but its ingredients vary as widely as the countries in which it's made. Chilis are always the primary ingredient, but the degree to which the mixture involves smoky, floral, or dried spices changes from place to place and house to house. Like many of the versions I've tasted in Morocco and France, ours has faint floral notes that come from lime, rose petals, and rose water, which you'll only taste toward the end of each bite, and then only if you're paying attention.

An 11-cup food processor is just big enough to hold this batch of harissa. If you have a smaller machine, split the work into two batches and blend them together at the end in a large bowl before storing.

For information on where to find the spices for this recipe, see Resources, page 293.

6 ounces dried guajillo chilis
3 ounces dried *ají amarillo* chilis
  (also sold as *ají mirasol*)
⅓ cup whole caraway seeds
¼ cup whole cumin seeds
2 tablespoons whole coriander
  seeds
1 tablespoon whole fennel seeds
⅓ head garlic (about 6 large
  cloves), peeled

2 teaspoons rose petals
1¼ to 1½ cups freshly squeezed
  lime juice (from about 10 to
  12 medium limes)
½ teaspoon rose water
½ cup extra-virgin olive oil, plus
  more for storing
2 to 3 tablespoons kosher salt

282

+ Place all the chilis in a large pot and add boiling water to cover. Over high heat, return the water to a boil, then remove the pot from the heat, weight the chilis with a smaller pan to ensure they're all submerged, and allow them to sit, covered, for about 24 hours, or until they are soft. (Depending on the chilis, it may not take this long; just make sure the skins are soft.)

+ Next, put the caraway, cumin, coriander, and fennel seeds in a large sauté pan over medium heat. Cook the seeds for a few minutes, stirring frequently, until they are toasted and fragrant, and some of them begin popping. Transfer the spices to a plate to cool.

+ When the spices have cooled, transfer them to the work bowl of a food processor, and whirl until the spices are ground almost to a powder. Add the garlic and rose petals, and pulse about 10 times to form a dry paste.

+ Working with gloves on if you're sensitive to spice, pull the stems out of the chilis and add the chilis to the food processor, along with any water that comes along for the ride. (Discard the stems, but reserve the chili cooking water; you may need it later.) Add 1¼ cups of the lime juice and the rose water, and whirl until the chilis are very finely chopped, stopping to scrape down the sides and top of the food processor as necessary. (Depending on your machine and your chilis, this may take 5 entire minutes of processing, so be patient. You're looking for the texture of small-curd cottage cheese.) If the mixture seems too thick to whirl around in the food processor, add some of the reserved chili water, about ¼ cup at a time, until the mixture moves.

+ When the chilis are finely chopped, add ½ cup of the olive oil and 2 tablespoons of the salt, and mix again to blend. Taste for seasoning, adding more of the remaining ¼ cup lime juice and 1 tablespoon salt, plus more again if desired. Transfer the harissa to a bowl and refrigerate, covered, for at least 1 day before using. To store, scoop it into pint-size jars, pour a thin layer of olive oil on top, and refrigerate for up to 2 months.

tapenade

PREP TIME: 10 MINUTES // TOTAL TIME: 10 MINUTES // MAKES 3 GENEROUS CUPS

I TYPICALLY USE OIL-CURED OLIVES FOR tapenade because they're earthier and less acidic than something like a Kalamata olive, but any dark olive will work. Serve the tapenade on grilled steak or with roasted chicken, or atop a tartine of Grilled Bread (page 277) and a delicious soft goat cheese.

3 cups pitted oil-cured olives
Julienned peel of half a medium
   lemon
¼ cup freshly squeezed lemon juice
   (from about 2 medium lemons)

1 tablespoon fresh thyme leaves
1 garlic clove, minced
1 cup extra-virgin olive oil, plus
   more for topping the tapenade

+ In the work bowl of a food processor, pulse the olives until roughly chopped. Add the lemon peel and juice, thyme leaves, and garlic, and pulse again a few times, until the olives are finely chopped. With the motor on, add the olive oil through the top of the machine, processing just until all the oil has been added. (The tapenade should still have some texture.)

+ Use immediately, or transfer the tapenade to an airtight container, cover with a thin layer of olive oil, and refrigerate for up to 1 month.

chermoula

CHERMOULA IS A NORTH AFRICAN SPICE mixture, often containing cumin, coriander, paprika, and red pepper flakes, traditionally used to season meat or fish. I love how the spices accent sweet root vegetables.

3 tablespoons cumin seeds,
toasted and ground

1 tablespoon coriander seeds,
toasted and ground

2 tablespoons smoked paprika

2 teaspoons red pepper flakes

5 cloves garlic, smashed

2 tablespoons freshly squeezed
lime juice (from about
1 medium lime)

1 teaspoon kosher salt

¼ teaspoon freshly ground black
pepper

½ cup extra-virgin olive oil

2 tablespoons water

✦ In the work bowl of a food processor or heavy-duty blender, whirl the ground cumin, ground coriander, paprika, and red pepper flakes to combine. Add the garlic, lime juice, salt, and pepper, and blend again until the garlic is finely chopped. With the motor running, add the olive oil in a slow, steady stream through the top of the machine, then add the water and process for a minute or two, until the mixture is well emulsified but there are still a few small pieces of spice left. Transfer the mixture to a glass jar and refrigerate, tightly sealed, until ready to use, up to 1 week.

crème fraîche

PREP TIME: 5 MINUTES // TOTAL TIME: 2 TO 3 DAYS // MAKES 1 QUART
SPECIAL EQUIPMENT: CHEESECLOTH

CRÈME FRAÎCHE IS THE DARLING OF the dairy aisle, and it fetches an equally dear price. Making your own is economically smart, but it's also delicious—and quicker than you might think. Start with good cultured buttermilk, not a combination of milk and vinegar.

3 cups heavy cream   1 cup buttermilk

→ In a mixing bowl, whisk together the cream and buttermilk. Cover the top of the bowl with 3 individual layers of cheesecloth (you can attach it to the bowl with a rubber band, if you're nervous it will fall off) and let the crème sit for 2 to 3 days, until thick. Gently stir it, then transfer the crème fraîche to an airtight container and refrigerate until ready to use, up to 1 week.

homemade yogurt

PREP TIME: 45 MINUTES, INCLUDING COOLING TIME
TOTAL TIME: ABOUT 24 HOURS // MAKES 2 QUARTS
SPECIAL EQUIPMENT: CHEESECLOTH, CANDY THERMOMETER

LIKE CRÈME FRAÎCHE, A GOOD, SILKY European yogurt can be quite expensive, so in the restaurants, we make our own. Since restaurant kitchens are naturally quite warm, ours thickens easily in a pot near the stove. At home, keep it in an area that's about 80 degrees Fahrenheit—a warm kitchen works, as does a floor with radiant heat. If your kitchen is cold, surround the pot with jars of hot water and cover the pot and jars with a big towel to create a warm area.

I also like how making my own yogurt allows me to control the texture, so if I want something a little thicker, I can strain it over cheesecloth until it reaches the perfect consistency. Note that the yogurt will thicken up a bit in the refrigerator.

½ gallon whole milk   ⅓ cup plain whole milk yogurt

+ In a large stainless-steel pot, heat the milk over medium heat until you see tiny bubbles at the edges, or until the milk reaches 185 degrees F on a candy thermometer, 15 to 20 minutes. Turn off the heat and let the milk cool down until it reaches 109 degrees F on a candy thermometer, about 30 minutes. Whisk the yogurt into the mixture, cover the pot with cheesecloth, and let the yogurt sit in a warm spot to thicken for about 24 hours. When the yogurt has reached a consistency you like, transfer it to sealed jars and refrigerate, or, if you prefer thicker yogurt, strain it for a few hours in a fine-mesh strainer lined with 4 or 5 layers of cheesecloth, then refrigerate. Serve chilled, or store it in the refrigerator for up to 1 week.

ricotta

PREP TIME: 20 MINUTES // TOTAL TIME: 1 HOUR 20 MINUTES // MAKES 1 CUP
SPECIAL EQUIPMENT: CHEESECLOTH, CANDY THERMOMETER

DON'T ASK WHY YOU WOULD MAKE your own ricotta—ask why you wouldn't make it. With good fresh milk and cream, the process takes a matter of minutes and results in fresh, creamy cheese perfect for just about everything, from spreading on breakfast toast to serving, slightly sweetened, with poached pears and a drizzle of walnut oil.

3 cups whole milk
1 cup heavy cream
1 teaspoon kosher salt

3 tablespoons freshly squeezed
    lemon juice (from about 1 large
    lemon)

➤ In a stainless-steel pot, stir together the milk, cream, and salt. Cook over medium-high heat, stirring occasionally with a spatula to prevent burning, until the mixture reaches 190 degrees F on a candy thermometer. Remove the pan from the heat, stir in the lemon juice, and let the mixture sit for 10 minutes, stirring gently every now and then.

➤ Set a fine-mesh strainer over a large bowl and line the strainer with 6 individual layers of cheesecloth, patting the cloth down so it lies flat in the strainer. Carefully pour the hot milk mixture into the cheesecloth and let drain for 1 hour. (Make sure the bottom of the strainer isn't sitting in any liquid.)

➤ Transfer the ricotta to a bowl, stir once or twice with a wooden spoon to fluff it, and refrigerate, covered, until ready to use, up to 1 week.

vanilla bean salt

PREP TIME: 5 MINUTES // TOTAL TIME: 5 MINUTES // MAKES: 2 CUPS

USE THIS FOR TOMATOES (PAGE 197) or to top your favorite ice cream.

1 cup flaky sea salt, such as Maldon
or Jacobsen (see Resources,
page 293)

2 whole vanilla beans

✦ Put the sea salt in a large mixing bowl. Using a small, sharp knife, split the
vanilla beans lengthwise. Scrape the beans' seeds into the salt, and stir them in
until well distributed. Add the pods, then transfer the salt to a sealable container,
such as a large glass jar. Store the salt at room temperature for at least a day
before using, and up to 3 months.

vanilla ice cream

PREP TIME: 30 MINUTES // TOTAL TIME: 24 HOURS (TO CHILL ICE CREAM)
MAKES ABOUT 1 QUART
SPECIAL EQUIPMENT: ICE CREAM MAKER

ONE OF MY FAVORITE THINGS IN the world is vanilla ice cream drizzled with grassy, peppery olive oil (see Choosing Olive Oil, page 11) and Vanilla Bean Salt (page 288). This version of vanilla ice cream, adapted from the recipe in David Lebovitz's book *The Perfect Scoop*, is my favorite.

1 cup whole milk
½ cup sugar
¼ teaspoon crushed flaky sea salt, such as Maldon or Jacobsen (see Resources, page 293)

1 whole vanilla bean, split lengthwise, seeds scraped out and reserved
6 large egg yolks
2 cups heavy cream
½ teaspoon vanilla extract

✦ In a medium saucepan, combine the milk, sugar, salt, and vanilla bean pod and seeds over medium heat. Cook until the milk is warm and the sugar has dissolved, whisking to disperse the vanilla beans evenly. Remove the pan from the heat and let it sit for 1 hour, so the vanilla flavor infuses into the milk.

✦ In a large glass or metal bowl, whisk the egg yolks until pale and thick. Rewarm the milk over medium heat until it begins to steam but doesn't simmer. Slowly pour the milk into the egg yolks, whisking constantly so the yolks don't cook.

✦ Put the heavy cream into another large bowl and set aside.

✦ Place the bowl with the egg mixture over a water bath, bring the water to a bare simmer, and cook the mixture over low heat until the custard thickens enough to coat the back of a rubber spatula, stirring constantly and scraping the bottom of the bowl with the spatula to prevent curdling.

✦ Using a fine-mesh strainer, strain the custard into the heavy cream and whisk to combine. (If you want, you can rinse off the used vanilla bean, let it dry completely, and stick it into a bag of sugar to give the sugar a light vanilla flavor.) Stir the mixture over an ice bath until cool (or let it cool in the refrigerator, stirring frequently), then mix in the vanilla extract. Chill overnight, if possible. Freeze the ice cream in an ice cream maker according to the manufacturer's instructions.

shirlee's crust

PREP TIME: 10 MINUTES // TOTAL TIME: 40 MINUTES // MAKES 2

RELIABLY, EVERY TIME I SIT FOR a moment at The Whale Wins, where we often serve thick, decadent chocolate brownies for dessert, I hear this question: Who is Shirlee, and why do we want her brownie? You want it because, like all her desserts, she's perfected it.

I'm not a sweets person, but desserts were still a big part of my life growing up. More than brownies, we ate pie. This is my mother's crust.

To make the crust for a tart, simply halve this recipe, or make it as is and freeze the leftover crust, well wrapped, for up to three months.

NOTE: This crust can also be made in a food processor. Pulse the flour, salt, and butter together about 20 times, until the butter is the size of small peas, then add the water while pulsing the machine. You've added enough water when the dough gathers up on the sides of the work bowl.

2½ cups (about 320 grams)
all-purpose flour, sifted
1 teaspoon kosher salt

1 cup (2 sticks) cold unsalted
butter, cut into 16 pieces
½ cup ice water, plus or minus a
tablespoon

✦ In a large bowl, whisk together the flour and salt. Add the butter pieces, and, using a pastry cutter, work the butter into the flour until the pieces are roughly the size of small peas. Using a fork, stir the water in a tablespoon at a time, adding just enough for the dough to stick together when pressed gently between your palms.

✦ Gently knead the dough into a ball, cut it in two, form each half into a disk, and wrap each in plastic wrap. Refrigerate until firm, at least 30 minutes, before using.

Resources

Here is a list of my preferred brands; most websites have ordering information. Amazon.com and ChefShop.com are also great general resources for most shelf-stable products. If you are in Seattle, many of the items below are available for purchase at The Whale Wins or Barnacle.

BOOZE

BOURBON: Buffalo Trace, BuffaloTrace.com

CALVADOS: Adrien Camut, KLWines.com

CIDER: Eric Bordelet, EricBordelet.com; Finnriver Farm & Cidery, Finnriver.com

COGNAC/ARMAGNAC: Courvoisier, Courvoisier.com; Tariquet, Tariquet.com

GIN: Voyager Dry Gin, PacificDistillery.com; Boodles British Gin, BoodlesGin.com; Big Gin, CaptiveSpiritsDistilling.com

SHERRY: Hidalgo La Gitana Manzanilla, Tienda.com; Lustau, KLWines.com

VERMOUTH: Dolin Vermouth de Chambéry, KLWines.com

VODKA: Stolichnaya, Stoli.com

WINES: K&L Wine Merchants, KLWines.com; Calvert Woodley Wine & Spirits, CalvertWoodley.com

DAIRY

BUTTER: Crémerie Classique brand, LarsensCreamery.com

CHEESE (ASSORTED): Murray's, MurraysCheese.com

CHEESE (CHEDDAR): Beecher's, BeechersHandmadeCheese.com

CRÈME FRAÎCHE AND RICOTTA: Bellwether Farms, BellwetherFarms.com

YOGURT: Straus, StrausFamilyCreamery.com

FISH AND SHELLFISH

ANCHOVIES (OIL-PACKED): Scalia brand, ChefShop.com

ANCHOVIES (SALT-PACKED): Scalia brand, ChefShop.com

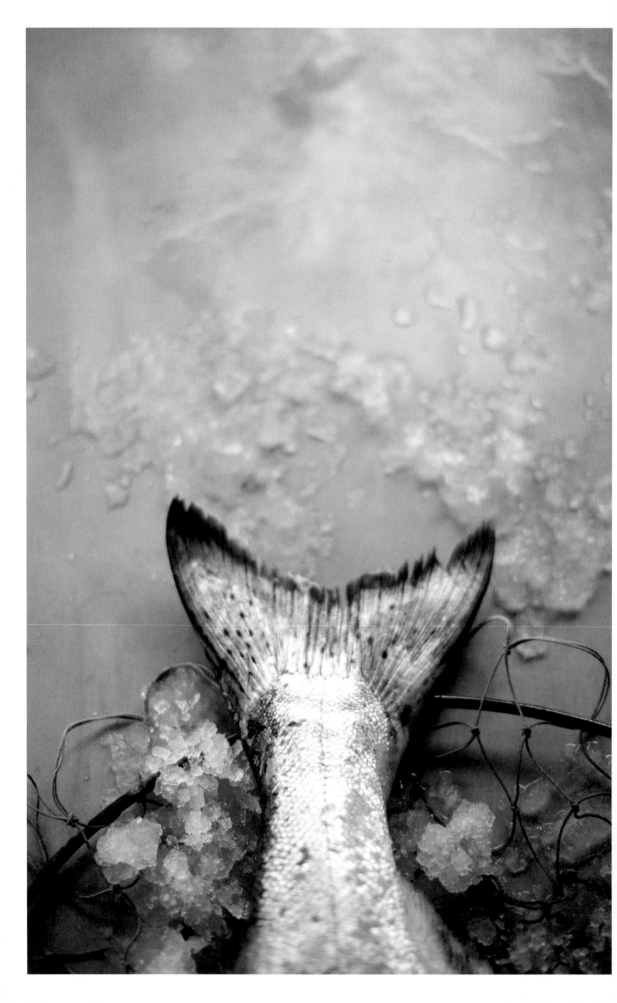

BOQUERONES: Coeur de la Mer brand, Heart-of-the-Sea.com

CANNED SARDINES: Ortiz brand, ChefShop.com; Matiz and Pollastrini di Anzio brands, Amazon.com

CLAMS, OYSTERS, SPOT PRAWNS: Hama Hama Oyster Company, HamaHamaOysters.com

CRABS, HALIBUT, MUSSELS, OCTOPUSES, SALMON, SCALLOPS, IKURA, OTHER ROE: I Love Blue Sea, ILoveBlueSea.com; Loki Fish Co., LokiFish.com

OCTOPUSES: Jones Family Farms, JFFarms.com

SMOKED SALMON: Gerard & Dominique Seafoods, GDSeafoods.com; ILoveBlueSea.com; and LokiFish.com

SPOT PRAWNS, FROZEN: Sylver Fishing Company (large and extra-large sizes, with roe if possible), PO Box 2281, Wrangell, AK 99929, (907) 874-2998

MEAT PRODUCTS

CAUL FAT: Marx Foods, MarxFoods.com, or your local butcher

DUCK FAT: D'Artagnan, dArtagnan.com, or your local butcher

PANTRY STAPLES

APPLE CIDER VINEGAR: Bragg or Spectrum brands, local grocery

BELUGA LENTILS: Zürsun Idaho Heirloom Beans, ZursunBeans.com

BOAT STREET PICKLES: BoatStreetPickles.com

CAPERS (BRINED): Roland brand, local grocery

CAPERS (SALT-PACKED): Agostino Recca brand, ChefShop.com

CHAMPAGNE VINEGAR: Beaufor brand (for dressings), FormaggioKitchen.com; Spectrum brand (for pickling), local grocery

DEMERARA SUGAR: India Tree, Amazon.com or ChefShop.com

HARISSA PASTE: The Fresh Olive Company, FreshOlive.com

HONEY: Ballard Bee Company, BallardBeeCompany.com

JAMS AND MARMALADES: Blue Chair Fruit Company, BlueChairFruit.com

KOSHER SALT: Diamond Crystal brand, local grocery

OLIVE OIL (GENERAL USE): Atlas Huile d'Olive Vierge Extra, ChefShop.com

OLIVE OILS (FINISHING): Capezzana brand (Tuscany), Atlas Les Terroirs de Marrakech brand (Morocco), olio nuovo (fresh-pressed olive oil), all available at ChefShop.com; Laudemio brand (Tuscany), Amazon.com

OLIVES: The Fresh Olive Company, FreshOlive.com

PRESERVED LEMONS: Mustapha's Moroccan Preserved Lemons, Mustaphas.com

PRESERVES: V Smiley Preserves, VSmileyPreserves.com

ROSE WATER: Nielsen Massey, Amazon.com

TURBINADO SUGAR: Woodstock Farms, Amazon.com

WALNUT OIL: J. LeBlanc brand, FormaggioKitchen.com

WHITE WINE VINEGAR: Beaufor brand (for dressings), FormaggioKitchen.com; Spectrum brand (for pickling), local grocery

VANILLA EXTRACT: Nielsen Massey Madagascar Bourbon Pure Vanilla, Amazon.com

PRODUCE

CHILI PEPPERS (SUCH AS PADRÓN): Viridian Farms, ViridianFarms.com

STONE FRUIT (APRICOTS, PEACHES, NECTARINES): Rama Farm, RamaFarm.com

SPICES

PIMENT D'ESPELETTE: Veridian Farms, VeridianFarms.com; World Spice Merchants, WorldSpice.com

SALTS, DRIED CHILIS, TELLICHERRY PEPPERCORNS, ROSE PETALS, ASSORTED SPICES: World Spice Merchants, WorldSpice.com

SEA SALT: Fleur de sel de Camargue, Jacobsen brand, Maldon brand, sel gris de Guérande, all available at The Meadow, AtTheMeadow.com

VANILLA BEANS: World Spice Merchants, WorldSpice.com

TABLEWARE

LINENS: Libeco, LibecoHomeStores.com

STONEWARE PLATES: Pillivuyt, PillivuytUS.com; Dudson, Dudson.com; Steelite International, Steelite.com

UNUSUAL FAVORITES

ANCHOVY-STUFFED OLIVES: La Novia del Sol brand, ChefShop.com

CALABRIAN CHILIS: Tutto Calabria brand, Amazon.com

HONEY VINEGAR: Il Miele della Vita brand, Manicaretti.com

MUSTARD SEED OIL: ChefShop.com

Index

Note: Photographs are indicated by *italics*.

A

Agrodolce, Onion, 40
Aioli, Garlic, 281
alcohol
    calvados, 247
    cider, 248
    Holiday Wines, 60–61
    resources, 293
    Rosé wines, 156, *170*, 171
    vermouth, 65
    Zetter Martini, 65
anchovies
    Anchovy Butter, 196
    Anchovy Vinaigrette, 174
    Boquerones Toasts, *72*, 73
    buying and preparing, 187–188, *189*
    Green Goddess Dressing, *190*, 191
    resources, 293, 295
    Tartine with Chili-Marinated Anchovies and
      Butter, 158–159, *159*
apples
    Apple Pie with Shirlee's Crust, 270
    Applesauce with Butter and Black Pepper, 270
    Baked Apples, 270
    with Braised Cabbage, 245
    Celery, Kohlrabi, Apple, and Walnut Salad,
      240–241, *241*
    French Apple Cake, *246*, 247–248
    Parsnip Soup, 237
    Raw Shaved Brussels Sprouts with Apples,
      Walnut Oil, and Black Pepper, 271
Artichokes, Steamed, *114*, 115
asparagus
    Asparagus with Julia's Blender Hollandaise
      and Chervil, 100
    Chilled Asparagus Soup with Yogurt, 100
    Raw Asparagus Salad, 116
    Roasted Asparagus with Mashed Avocado,
      Poached Egg, and Mustard Seed Oil, 100

B

Baguette Toasts, 278
Barnacle, *5*, 6
bay leaves, as flavoring for pickles, 225, *226*

beans, fava
    Fava Bean, Pea, and Spring Onion Potato
      Salad with Mint, 101
    Grilled Whole Favas over Ricotta with Honey,
      Lime, and Aleppo Pepper, 101
    Puréed Favas with Olive and Garlic, 101
beef
    Grilled Dry-Aged Rib-Eye Steaks, *194*,
      195–196
    Roasted Marrow Bones, 253–254, *255*
    Standing Rib Roast, 49–51, *50*
    Steak Tartare, *66*, 67
Beets, Grilled, *162*, 163–165
Beets, Pickled, 223
berries
    Blackberry Cobbler, 180
    Blackberry Eton Mess, 180
    Blackberry Jam with Fresh Bay, 23
    Meringues with Apricots, Berries, and Cream,
      175–176, *177*
    Red Wine–Blackberry Syrup, 180
    Strawberry Jam Tart, 98–99, *99*
    Strawberry Shortcake, 151–153, *152*, *153*
Birthday, My, 185–203
Boat Street Bread Pudding, *58*, 59–60
Boat Street Café, *2*, *3*, 6,
Boat Street Chicken Liver Pâté, 74–75, *75*
Boat Street Cream Scones, 20–23, *21*
Boquerones Toasts, *72*, 73
bread and bread dishes
    Boat Street Bread Pudding, *58*, 59–60
    Grilled Bread, 277
    Homemade Bread Crumbs, 276
    Strata, *28*, 29–30
    Walnut Tarator, 166–167, *167*
    Watermelon Panzanella, 180
    Zucchini Bread, 267–269, *268*
    See also toasts
brussels sprouts
    Deep-Fried Brussels Sprouts with Salt,
      Chives, and Piment d'Espelette, 270–271
    Raw Shaved Brussels Sprouts with Apples,
      Walnut Oil, and Black Pepper, 271
    Roasted Brussels Sprouts Carbonara with
      Cayenne, 271
butters
    Anchovy Butter, 196
    Brown Butter Vinaigrette, 260
    Harissa Butter, 142
    Herring Butter, 68, *69*
    Snail Butter, *88*, 89–90, *90*

Conversions

VOLUME			LENGTH		WEIGHT	
UNITED STATES	METRIC	IMPERIAL	UNITED STATES	METRIC	AVOIRDUPOIS	METRIC
¼ tsp.	1.25 ml		⅛ in.	3 mm	¼ oz.	7 g
½ tsp.	2.5 ml		¼ in.	6 mm	½ oz.	15 g
1 tsp.	5 ml		½ in.	1.25 cm	1 oz.	30 g
½ tbsp.	7.5 ml		1 in.	2.5 cm	2 oz.	60 g
1 tbsp.	15 ml		1 ft.	30 cm	3 oz.	90 g
⅛ c.	30 ml	1 fl. oz.			4 oz.	115 g
¼ c.	60 ml	2 fl. oz.			5 oz.	150 g
⅓ c.	80 ml	2.5 fl. oz.			6 oz.	175 g
½ c.	125 ml	4 fl. oz.			7 oz.	200 g
1 c.	250 ml	8 fl. oz.			8 oz. (½ lb.)	225 g
2 c. (1 pt.)	500 ml	16 fl. oz.			9 oz.	250 g
1 qt.	1 l	32 fl. oz.			10 oz.	300 g

TEMPERATURE				WEIGHT	
OVEN MARK	FAHRENHEIT	CELSIUS	GAS	AVOIRDUPOIS	METRIC
				11 oz.	325 g
Very cool	250–275	130–140	½–1	12 oz.	350 g
Cool	300	150	2	13 oz.	375 g
Warm	325	165	3	14 oz.	400 g
Moderate	350	175	4	15 oz.	425 g
Moderately hot	375	190	5	16 oz. (1 lb.)	450 g
	400	200	6	1½ lb.	750 g
Hot	425	220	7	2 lb.	900 g
	450	230	8	2¼ lb.	1 kg
Very Hot	475	245	9	3 lb.	1.4 kg
				4 lb.	1.8 kg

About the Authors

RENEE ERICKSON owned her first restaurant at age twenty-five. Today, with a fabulous staff, she runs four Seattle restaurants (Boat Street Café, The Walrus and the Carpenter, The Whale Wins, and Barnacle) as well as Boat Street Pickles and Narwhal, an oyster truck. Her recipes have been featured in the *Wall Street Journal*, *Bon Appétit*, and *Food & Wine*. In 2014, she was a James Beard Award finalist for Best Chef: Northwest. This is her first cookbook.

JESS THOMSON is a Seattle-based food and travel writer and recipe developer, the author of the blog *hogwash*, and the winner of the 2012 MFK Fisher Award. She has written six cookbooks, including *Pike Place Market Recipes* and *Dishing Up Washington*.

About the Photographer

JIM HENKENS is a food and lifestyle photographer who splits his time between Seattle and Lummi Island, WA. When he isn't shooting for clients like Sur la Table, *Sunset* magazine, Nordstrom, and Starbucks, you'll find him searching for antique props or throwing sticks on the beach for his dog. This is his fifth cookbook.